the knot GUIDE FOR THE
MOTHER OF THE BRIDE

the knot GUIDE FOR THE MOTHER OF THE BRIDE

BY CARLEY RONEY

ILLUSTRATIONS BY
CINDY LUU

CHRONICLE BOOKS
SAN FRANCISCO

Library of Congress Cataloging-in-Publication Data available.

ISBN 0-8118-4636-9

Manufactured in China.

Book and cover design by Aufuldish & Warinner.

Distributed in Canada by Raincoast Books
9050 Shaughnessy Street
Vancouver, British Columbia V6P 6E5

10 9 8 7 6 5 4 3 2 1

Chronicle Books LLC
85 Second Street
San Francisco, California 94105

www.chroniclebooks.com

ACKNOWLEDGMENTS

I AM EXTREMELY FORTUNATE to work with such a talented and dedicated staff at The Knot. Thank you to all who contributed, from checking our etiquette to adding an artful turn of phrase—and a special thanks to Kathleen Murray and Rosie Amodio, who helped pull it all together.

This book would not have been possible without the insight of the thousands of brides and moms who log on to The Knot Web site every day and share their stories of love, excitement, anxiety, and relief. There was no better source for learning about the evolving relationship between a bride and her mother.

More special thanks: To the team at Chronicle, especially our editor, Mikyla Bruder, for her advice, patience, and inspiring vision. To Cindy Luu, for her delightful illustrations. To Victoria Colby, for her great eye. And to Jennifer Unter, for crossing all the T's.

Thanks and love to my family, David, Havana, Cairo, and Nai Nai.

And a closing hug and kiss to my very own mother of the bride, who stood lovingly by my side as I prepared to walk down the aisle.

[INTRODUCTION]

We understand how exciting it is for a mother when something as wonderful as marriage happens to her daughter—watching your baby girl become a blushing bride is an exhilarating, once-in-a-lifetime experience. And chances are, as soon as you heard your daughter's wonderful news, your mind quickly turned to doing anything and everything possible to help give her the wedding of her dreams. Your first smart move: picking up this book. It's an up-to-date guide to wedding planning written with mothers of the bride in mind. As you might have noticed, today's weddings are a bit different from those when you were a bride. These days, the rule of thumb is that there are no rules. Many brides and grooms marry older, contribute to or even pay for the celebration themselves, and put their own personal stamp on the affair.

All this modernity leaves today's mother of the bride with the ultimate challenge: being supportive yet not overbearing, helping out without taking control, and learning when to bite her tongue and when to stand up for her little girl's decisions. Your daughter will probably want your approval and your know-how to pull it all together, but she will always want to feel that it's her party. A word of advice to begin this book: share your best advice, but don't try to oversell your ideas. Ask people you trust for great caterer or band recommendations, but then let your daughter figure out whom she wants to meet; disclose your concerns about mismatching bridesmaid dresses, but then express your surprised delight when they come out all right (even if you don't think they did!).

Throughout this book, we provide you with all the information that you, as the mother of the bride—or MOB—really need to know. In chapter 1, we begin by explaining the first key wedding-planning steps, including engagement announcement etiquette, tackling the guest list, and deciding whether to throw an engagement party (P.S.: it's totally up to you). Then we make sure you're communicating properly with all the parties involved (you want to start things right) and share our step-by-step strategy for figuring out the wedding budget. From there, chapter 2 walks you through the planning process from start to finish, pointing out specific instances when you can lend a helping hand (such as taking charge of the RSVPs) and times when you should offer wise words of encouragement or creative cost-cutting ideas to your daughter. We also help you discover your MOB style and decide how involved in the planning you (and your daughter!) want to be. And, finally, we keep you on track with our detailed timeline of those crucial last-minute to-dos before the main event.

Breathe a sigh of relief, because chapter 3 is all about you. We give you all the tools you need to make yourself beautiful, with tips on how to complement the wedding's style with your own look, find the perfect dress to flatter your figure, and even where to start shopping. Plus, we shower you with solid beauty advice to take years off your skin, tricks to help you light up the camera lens, and fail-safe tactics to get you in shape for the big day.

While we're on the topic of prep work, chapter 4 is the ultimate hostess's companion, clarifying the ins and outs of prewedding parties. From the shower to the day-after brunch, we let you know what your role should be in each event, offer great gift-giving ideas, and reveal ways you can pitch in (such as letting your friends know where your darling is registered) even when you're not hosting the event.

Finally, chapter 5 covers what all the other chapters lead up to: the big day. We give you excellent advice on how to get everyone to the chapel on time and looking beautiful, what you should expect during the ceremony (besides tears of joy!), receiving-line essentials, and, most important, how to enjoy yourself all night long—and create treasured memories. Web-savvy ladies can also head to www.theknot.com/mob for our most current information on invitation wording, mother-of-the-bride dresses, local wedding-gown preservationists, and a personal guest-manager tool that enables you to track RSVPs with ease.

Let's face it: Even though we all know that weddings are about love, it's way too easy to become overly concerned about impressing people with a fabulous party. We're here to help you avoid that pitfall and to celebrate the joy of being the mother of the bride, all the while keeping you calm, cool, collected, and looking your most fabulous ever. A wedding is a wonderful experience for a mother and her daughter, so make the most of it—together.

WHERE TO BEGIN

LET US GUESS: You're awash in a million ideas, from where to have the wedding to which band is the best in town. Planning, we all know, can be pretty overwhelming. And planning a wedding—with all the emotion involved—can be intense. But it can also be wonderful, and it's important to remember that, from now until the very last moments of that impeccably executed party. So before you (both) start to drown in the details, let's get organized.

In this chapter, we give you the tools to tackle the first month of the planning timeline. We explain the etiquette of the engagement period, with pointers on how to spread the word as well as engagement party must-dos. Then we show you the best way to draw up a guest list—the most essential planning task for any wedding—and share important advice on deciding how involved an MOB you plan to be. Then we assist you in opening lines of communication with your daughter, your future son-in-law, and, of course, his parents. Finally, we'll teach you and your daughter to create a working wedding budget together. Starting things right will set a healthy, happy tone for the rest of your planning days.

THE RULES OF ENGAGEMENT

SPREADING THE NEWS

You were probably one of the very first people to hear about the proposal—if your daughter's fellow is a traditional guy, you might even have known before she did. Now it's your turn to be the bearer of good news. Just keep one crucial detail in mind: The people you ring up at this point most likely will expect a wedding invitation. So choose carefully, but don't feel that you have to keep her engagement confidential. Instead, let the happy news gel, and wait for word of mouth to take its natural course. Your goal is to avoid guaranteeing anyone (besides your immediate family) a spot on the guest list, and thus to prevent hurt feelings later.

Share this noncommittal tactic with your daughter before you both start calling important relatives. You should also prepare a tactful response in case people begin to press the guest-list issue. Being ambiguous about details will often get you out of sticky situations, such as when Cousin Caroline says she can't wait for her adorable son to be the ringbearer at a big formal wedding, while your daughter has visions of a small destination wedding in Italy. Your response to curious folk? You're "not sure what she has in mind" or "how many people you're expecting." The truth works.

After you've put the phone to rest, there are several ways to announce the engagement to everyone else. Public proclamations in hometown newspapers usually appear quickly and are a problem-guest-free way to share the news. Usually, engagement notices come from the "host" of the wedding, so speak with the happy couple and make sure they're comfortable with you assuming this role of honor. Call the publications, such as your local newspaper, where you want the announcement to appear, and ask for a standardized form, if available, and the publication's announcement guidelines. Space permitting, newspaper announcements include the bride's or groom's parents' names and places of residence (sometimes both are listed—it depends on which paper you submit the announcement to), plus details on the couple's career and educational background. Find out if there's a publication fee and whether the paper accepts pictures. Some papers have strict photo standards (for example, the couple's eyebrows must be at the same height), so you and the bridal couple might want to discuss setting up an engagement photo session. The groom's parents should call their community paper. Other publications to consider are high school and college alumni newsletters or magazines—generally, your daughter should take care of these arenas.

If you plan to mail a printed engagement announcement, first consider who's on the guest list. Visit a stationery store with your daughter and look through traditional printed cards, or banish the cookie-cutter look by picking creative stationery. If the timing's right, you could also include the announcement in your annual holiday cards and spread good cheer during a hectic time of the year.

Finally, although you might consider e-mail an uncouth mode of communication, sending an engagement announcement via the Internet is perfectly acceptable and probably the best route for informing your daughter's friends and your close family and friends who live outside the country. But we can't promise that your phone won't ring off the hook with well wishers later!

Need a helping hand in finalizing your daughter's engagement announcement? Here are some standard wordings for you and your daughter to choose from.

HOSTS: YOU AND YOUR HUSBAND

Mr. and Mrs. John Doe of Chicago announce the engagement of their daughter, Jane, to Jack Smith, son of Bill and Joan Smith of Englewood, New Jersey. Ms. Doe, a graduate of Vassar College, is a professor at Barnard College in New York City. Mr. Smith graduated magna cum laude from Columbia Law School and works at Smith, Golden, his mother's law firm, in Fort Lee, New Jersey. A June wedding is planned. [Or: No date has yet been set for the wedding.]

HOST: YOU

Ms. Janet Jones announces the engagement of her daughter, Jane Doe, to Jack Smith. . . . Ms. Doe is also the daughter of John Doe of Sioux City. [The latter sentence is placed close to the end of the announcement.]

HOSTS: YOU AND A NEW SPOUSE

Ms. Janet Jones and Mr. Timothy Chapin announce the engagement of Ms. Jones's daughter, Jane Doe, to Jack Smith. . . . Ms. Doe is also the daughter of John Doe of Sioux City.

HOST: YOU (HER FATHER IS DECEASED)

The engagement of Jane Annette Doe, daughter of Mrs. Janet Doe and the late Mr. John Doe, to Jack Smith, son of Bill and Joan Smith of Englewood, New Jersey, is announced by the bride's mother. . . .

HOSTS: THE COUPLE

Jane Doe, a professor at Barnard College, is to be married to Jack Smith, a partner at the law firm of Smith, Golden in Fort Lee, New Jersey. Ms. Doe is the daughter of Mr. John Doe of Sioux City, Iowa, and Ms. Janet Jones of Chicago. Mr. Smith is. . . .

THE ENGAGEMENT PARTY

Once all your nearest and dearest hear about your daughter's engagement, you might feel the urge to gather everyone together to toast the devoted duo. Tradition has it that the bride's parents host the initial gathering, but whether you throw an engagement party is entirely up to you. If you choose to do so, there are two ways you can go. If you don't know your daughter's soon-to-be in-laws and the couple's closest friends, this might be a lovely time to get them together, bonding at a small and intimate affair. On the other hand, you can consider this your chance to set the tone for the upcoming nuptials with a celebration to top all celebrations. As you decide, here's what you, as the mother of the bride, should keep in mind:

Give the couple time to breathe. An impromptu family gathering the weekend after he proposed is the perfect opportunity to break out the vintage champagne, but don't schedule an all-out opulent affair during the engagement's first month. Plan to host an engagement party two to four months after he slid on that diamond ring. That gives the couple a chance to envision their eventual wedding—a crucial element to consider when deciding on the type of event you will throw.

Find out the size of the wedding that your daughter and her fiancé have in mind. Everyone who is invited to the engagement party should ultimately be invited to the wedding. That said, if the couple decides to host their own wedding and keep the list small and you want to throw an extravagant engagement party, go for it. Just be sure to let people know that the wedding will be small so no feelings will be hurt when guests aren't invited to the wedding. If you are worried that your friends will think you want to have a big bash solely to shower your daughter with gifts, include a nice note in the invitation that requests no presents.

Consider what will make your soon-to-be son-in-law's family most comfort-able. Since the engagement party custom was actually designed to help you start building bridges between the families, consider their style. If they are a very formal family, an impromptu picnic in the park might not be the most appropriate setting for getting to know one another. Settle nerves by including as many people from their side as you can reasonably accommodate.

Suggest that the couple register beforehand. While traditionally guests have not brought presents to this function, increasing numbers do today, and it's only fair to provide guidance. Remind the couple to register for gifts in the low to middle range—a five-hundred-dollar cappuccino maker is not your typical engagement present. If some guests arrive bearing gifts, just be sure the couple unwraps them *after* the party or away from the crowd so people who came empty-handed won't feel uncomfortable.

Remind yourself that there is still a wedding to throw. Every mother of the bride wants to host an unforgettable affair, but you never want to upstage the main event. If your guests are up to it, set off a black-tie affair with a sit-on-the-floor, buffet-style engagement bash; preview a semiformal daytime wedding with a swanky cocktail party, ties optional; or balance a destination wedding with a home-cooked dinner party.

ENGAGEMENT PARTY STARTERS

Whether you want to stage a simple soiree or a lavish celebration, these four engagement party ideas will get you thinking.

1. **JUST DESSERTS**
   Celebrate the sweethearts with a champagne-and-dessert-only fete. Serve up a selection of sumptuous sweets that guests can grab by the slice, such as white chocolate cheesecake, tiramisu, and red velvet cake. Monogrammed truffles and personalized cookies (in the shapes of a diamond ring, wedding cake, and gown) are perfect toasting treats. Flavored coffees and espresso drinks will leave everyone with a warm, fuzzy feeling.

2. **CHIC CLAMBAKE**
   Even if you don't live on the water, there's no reason you can't have a seafood-infused soiree. Create your own raw bar with fabulous finger food such as shrimp cocktail, king crabs' legs, oysters, and clams. Keep it cool with classic New England cocktails such as the Cape Codder (vodka and cranberry juice) or Sea Breeze (vodka and grapefruit and cranberry juices).

3. **WINE AND DINE**
   You can either throw a party at a local winery, have a sommelier come to your home to lead a wine tasting, or host a tasting at a restaurant, where a wine steward will do the honors. Send guests home with a personalized and young (and consequently inexpensive) bottle and instructions to open it on the date it will be aged to perfection; and present the happy couple with bottles to uncork on their fifth, tenth, and twenty-fifth anniversaries.

4. **LOVERS' LANE**
   If love is in the air, why not amp it up with an aphrodisiac feast? Chocolate, oysters, passion fruit . . . the works. Or salute the primary color of passion with a "simply red" spread that includes spicy drinks (red wine, cranberry cocktails, amber ales) and in-the-mood food (red pepper spread, tomato salad, red velvet cake).

SURVIVING THE GUEST LIST

It might seem a bit early to start listing potential wedding invitees, but, as we've already said, much revolves around this key list, and it's essential to engagement etiquette. Expect to start playing this name game in the first two months after the couple has decided to marry. Once unquestionably the purview of the bride's parents (who also planned and paid for the wedding), finessing the guest list now is a job probably best handled by the bride and groom. Technically, if you're paying for the reception, you have final say over how many guests are invited and how many the groom's side may invite, but there are so many variables and this is such a tricky, important job that there are no hard and fast rules. It's best to base the list on a formula that everyone agrees to (drawing the line at first cousins, for instance). Not only does this help prevent hurt feelings, it gives you a great out when you're forced to explain why someone was left off the list.

With these loose guidelines in place, start to think about your wish list—everyone you would invite in a perfect world with an unlimited amount of space. Share this strategy with your daughter, her fiancé, and his parents and ask them to make their own lists. It's much easier to cut the total list once you have an idea of the numbers you're talking about. You never know—maybe the groom comes from a small family and you will be able to include everyone you hope to invite. That said, be realistic about your invitees—don't lose credibility with your daughter by adding your hair-dresser to the mix.

We suggest that you categorize this "dream list." Common subsections include your immediate relatives and extended family to whom you're closest; your best friends and couples who have seen every one of your daughter's ballet recitals or soccer games; other good friends and neighbors who at least are familiar with her vital stats (where she lives, what she does, her fiancé's name); and faraway family members who might be offended if they're not invited. This will help you when and if it comes time to cut: for instance, you might decide to eliminate all co-workers across the board.

One note: It might seem totally tactless, but there's no steadfast rule that says you must offer reciprocal invitations to those who have invited you to weddings. Circumstances always change.

[GUEST LIST GAFFES]

When you start to compile your part of the guest list, avoid these pitfalls.

You assume faraway friends or family members won't come. If you're faced with space constraints or budget concerns, don't ever discount the possibility of someone traveling to the celebration from a far distance. They may see your daughter's wedding as an opportunity for a vacation, and gladly take you up on your invitation. On average, 10 to 20 percent of invitees probably won't attend—but you never want to rely on those figures.

You invite out-of-town guests who can't possibly attend. On the flip side, if it's pretty much guaranteed that a friend can't make the trip due to financial concerns, health issues, or even a fear of flying, you don't want to insinuate that your daughter (and you!) are looking for a gift. Consider mailing a wedding announcement instead. Of course, there are always some who might be offended by the invitation omission, so always be sure to invite your closest family and friends no matter where they live.

You send an invitation to an estranged family member in hopes of mending a riff. Let's clarify this: We're not saying don't invite an estranged relative, but rather, if you choose to renew the relationship, don't extend the wedding invitation out of the blue. The invitation won't solve the problem—only a candid discussion will do that.

Your best bet is to create an electronic spreadsheet that lists names, number of people in each party, and the category into which they fall. This way, you can easily tally your count and sort guests alphabetically or by category. Or simply type up a numbered list on your computer so you can add (and delete) people with ease.

Once the couple, the future in-laws, and you have scribed your ideal invitee lists, it's time to merge and purge. You and your daughter should figure out the wedding's target number or the approximate total invitees—the chosen venue and budget generally dictate this based on how many people will fit into the selected space and how much you are able (or willing) to spend per person. Remember that about 10 to 20 percent of your invitees won't be able to attend—and that figure will be much higher if the list is filled with out-of-towners or significantly lower if it's mainly locals.

Then determine how to divide your target number among yourselves. One egalitarian tactic is for the couple (or the couple and the bride's family, if they are paying for the wedding) to divide the number three ways, between the two families and the couple themselves. Another option: The couple draws up their own list that includes the family and family friends on both sides whom they want to have at the wedding, then allots each set of parents a number of invitees that the parents can add to the list. This strategy is gaining in popularity, since it stands to reason that couples want some say over whom they want to share their special day.

Most invitees should be people you mutually agree upon anyway, but if you feel obligated to include dear friends your daughter doesn't know well, ask her to streamline her list of people she rarely speaks to in order to make a little room—or offer to pay for the extra heads. Just be sure to keep these extra invitees to a handful of couples who will be appreciative and help you have a good time. Overinviting might make the couple feel that it's your affair, not theirs.

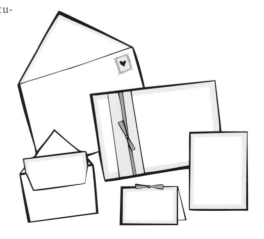

GUEST-LIST ETIQUETTE 101

Here are solutions for common guest-list problems.

AN OFFENDED B-LISTER

We're all for creating A and B guest lists. If you're pretty sure your cousins in Calgary won't be able to make it but you must invite them, put them on your A list, but keep a group of potential invitees on standby on a B list. It's a great way to include people whom you would love to invite but for whom you just don't seem to have room. Now, if you do get a chance to invite B-listers and they realize their late inclusion, just be honest with them. Explain the guest-list guidelines your families established and say you are thrilled to be able to celebrate your daughter's wedding with this person.

MIFFED PARENTS

If you decide to keep the wedding child-free, prepare a response for parents in case they ask to bring children anyway (all the while remembering that it really is out of line for them to question your and your family's guest-list moves). Don't be afraid to simply say that children are the cut-off point the two families have chosen. If you find that this is a problem—for example, guests are coming from far away and are uncomfortable leaving children with someone overnight—you might consider hiring one or two sitters to take care of kids in another room at your reception site.

DIVORCED COUPLES

If a couple very close to you and your husband has recently split, deciding whom to invite can be very difficult. As in most cases of divorce, consider the circumstances. If it's an amicable separation, invite them both but seat them at different tables. Or separately evaluate your and your daughter's relationship with each person—are you both closer to one of them? If it's a truly tricky situation, it might be best to speak with each person honestly.

CO-WORKERS

You spend most of your days with your co-workers. But even if you work in a small place and have made lifelong friends there, you might not be able to invite them all. Make it clear early that you don't have room to invite the whole office, and tell the one or two invited people (such as your boss) to keep their invitation low-profile.

THE FAMILY BOND

COMMUNICATING WITH YOUR DAUGHTER

Have you already envisioned the ideal wedding for your daughter? Perhaps something close to home, very elegant, and held in the place of worship where you exchanged your own vows? Well, we're betting that the bride-to-be has a binder packed with some entirely different vision. At the get-go, have a heart-to-heart with your daughter about the overall role you will play in the planning—you don't want to ever make her feel that you're running the show, unless that's exactly what she hopes for. (We explain all the nuances of your role and planning tasks in chapter 2.)

Without being overbearing, share with her the advice that you're dying to give her, everything that you've learned from being a mom and hostess all these years—and be prepared to listen, really *listen*, to her ideas for the wedding. Remember that your excited description of your vision might come off as if you have the wedding mapped out from start to finish—give her room to create the wedding of her dreams. You never know—maybe she will realize that mother does know best.

During this initial chat, decide how the two of you will proceed with the planning. There are three main possibilities here. One, your daughter wants you to take control of organizing the event; two, she wants to handle everything herself; or, three, you do it together. Ask yourself this: Do you want to be involved each and every step of the way, from calling the limo company to choosing the calligrapher? Do you want a say in the final design decisions? Are you looking to be the sole wedding planner? If so, and if your daughter is appreciative of your help, you're good to go. But if party planning just isn't your passion, speak up now or, as they say, forever hold your peace. Your daughter might say she wants a simple wedding, but that doesn't always entail a simple list of things to do. Or maybe she wants her own clear-cut vision to drive the event. If you're both happy with her taking on the task, terrific.

Even if you consider your daughter the perfect child, you're bound to brawl at some point in the planning. Here are the top four reasons that every good mom–bride team squabbles.

1. *Planning* any *big event is stressful*. This should go without saying, but people tend to forget that throwing a wedding is a little like producing a TV show, planning a lavish cocktail affair, and hosting a gigantic dinner party—all at once. (Never mind the rehearsal dinner, engagement parties, showers, and so on.)

2. *You have different dreams for the day*. Of course, we *know* you don't fit the stereotype of the controlling über-hostess who considers a daughter's wedding her grand opportunity to rise in the social standings. But you probably have a *few* (teensy-weensy!) expectations that clash with your darling daughter's.

3. *She's bound to act out* . . . Remember her twos, her teens, that year before college? Doubtless you won't get through this transition, either, without a few growing pains. A wedding is an emotionally vulnerable time for a young woman, and if she is going to lash out at someone, who do *you* think that person will be?

4. *. . . and so are you*. Since most young women now get married after living on their own for a while, we tend to forget that mothers are still, in a sense, giving away their daughters. To some extent, many MOBs see this as the last opportunity for a little control, a last chance to reinforce everything they've tried to teach their daughters.

Now, the third situation is the most common *and* the most complicated. If you decide to plan the wedding together, figure out your boundaries. When generations (and tastes) collide, things can get thorny. The best strategy is to ask her which aspect of the wedding she cares about most, so you'll know where to give up control. Your daughter should ask you the same. For instance, if you really can't bear the thought of mahi-mahi as a main dish but are willing to forgo the traditional ecru invitations, let this be known.

With so many people involved in the process (we'll get to the groom's side in a minute), it's not easy to please everyone. But the most important thing, above all the decisions about flowers and song lists, is to relish this time with your little one—remember, she'll be a bride only once.

THE SECRET TO YOUR SON-IN-LAW

You were always the one in your daughter's life who taught her right from wrong, who was there to bandage boo-boos, who cheered her on at cheerleading. Now there's a new influence around: her fiancé. He's her best friend and her confidant— and he's now a part of your life, too. We hope that you couldn't be happier, that you've recognized that this man cares deeply for your daughter. If so, show it.

Some parents already know their future son-in-law extremely well—especially if he's been around since high school. Parents who live far from their daughter and aren't as familiar with her betrothed can call him directly and welcome him into the family or send a nice note that expresses happiness for their marriage.

Clichés aside, it's no small thing to welcome a new member into the family. Suddenly it's not just your daughter's desires you have to take into account, but your soon-to-be son-in-law's approval as well. In the long run, you're better off taking him under your wing. First, garner from the groom-to-be what role he wants to play in the wedding. And remember, he has a set of parents to look out for as well, so if the two of you can work together happily, your families will do nothing but flow.

MEET THE PARENTS

Next up: It's time to meet his parents. Think of this meeting as a pure reflection of your happiness and love for your daughter and her new life. Tradition calls for them to first contact you and introduce themselves—but it's also perfectly acceptable for you and your husband to make the first move. (Note: If his parents are divorced, call on the parent[s] who raised him; when in doubt, contact his mom unless he is estranged from her.) The conversation can be as long or short as feels comfortable; its main purpose is to establish a plan to meet, so have a suggestion ready. If they live nearby, pick a time and a neutral place for everyone to gather—Sunday brunch or an informal dinner is the best way to encourage conversation, and it also establishes a set time limit for the meeting. If his parents reside in another part of the country, make an effort to find a convenient time to get together prior to the wedding. Otherwise, send a sincere letter conveying your excitement about the joining of the families. If the wedding is in your neck of the woods, invite them to check out the area and scope out rehearsal-dinner locations with the kids. This will supply something to talk about when you meet and will distract them from any differences you might have!

When the time comes to get together, your daughter might be fraught with nerves. Try to calm her fears with a relaxed attitude and a promise to avoid topics of potentially big conversation conflict, such as religion, politics, and sex. Remind your husband to steer clear of wedding-cost talk—make the fiancé's parents feel comfortable by setting up another time to discuss their financial involvement in the wedding. And we're sure we don't need to tell you this, but refrain from discussing your daughter's exes or telling any embarrassing stories—you need her on your side!

What conversation topics does that leave you? Ask questions about the family, their hometown, or their other (if any) children. Ahead of time, ask your daughter if she knows of any common interests to chat about, such as travel or baseball. If not, bring up something that both families share: your children, who are in love. Bring the betrothed into the conversation

(they often take the reins anyway) and focus on them for a bit. Above all, maintain your sense of humor and remember that even though his parents will soon be family, it's not imperative to become best friends—you just need to get along.

⌐CURBING SIBLING RIVALRY⌐

What to do when that deep-down fear of playing favorites seems to rear its ugly head? You've been spending every free minute on the phone with the bride-to-be, leaving her siblings suffering from a simple case of envy. Here are some hints on confronting the conflicts.

1. If the jealous son or daughter is married, point out that he or she has had the spotlight and should understand that you're spending time with the bride-to-be to put together the best wedding possible. When comparing weddings (and costs!) becomes an issue, explain that you tried to give your son/daughter the perfect wedding and now are doing the same for this child.

2. For those who haven't made the trip down the aisle, reassure them that their time is coming and that they will be lavished with all the attention that your daughter is receiving. Try to plan a day for just the two of you, without any mention of the wedding—a shopping spree always does the trick.

3. Including your other children in the wedding plans makes them feel like insiders, not outsiders. Give them special responsibilities, if it's okay with the bride, such as scoping out bridesmaid dress designers and booking appointments for the three of you. This will make your other daughter feel that it's her special day, too.

4. On the days leading up to the wedding, a small gift will remind them that you haven't forgotten them. Pick out something sentimental, such as Grandma's earrings or Grandpa's cufflinks, or something simple, such as a CD they've coveted.

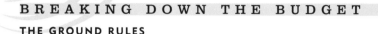

BREAKING DOWN THE BUDGET

THE GROUND RULES

Talking about money is never easy. And these days, there are no longer clear-cut answers to the question of who pays for what: at the very least, couples usually expect to contribute to and have some control over their nuptials. And, to be honest, with the average wedding now costing more than a new car, fewer families can afford to go it alone. Grooms' families are now often expected (and happy) to cover more than just the rehearsal dinner and a few boutonnieres. Keep such differences in mind, and be sure to ask the groom ahead of time so you do not offend his family.

Start by setting up a sit-down within the first few weeks of their engagement: Ask your daughter and your soon-to-be son-in-law if you can talk about how you can best contribute to the wedding. Be frank—let them know the discussion will be about money. We bet the couple (not to mention the in-laws) will breathe a huge sigh of relief when you broach the subject. The quicker you establish the budget basics, the freer everyone will feel to focus on the good stuff.

THE WAY TO PAY

Honestly, it's all about what works best for you and yours. Just follow our simple prescription to come up with a customized (and thoroughly modern) plan that makes everyone comfortable, and soon you and your darling can turn to what really matters: making her wedding—and the months leading up to it—a warm and loving time you'll still talk about when it's time for *her* wee ones to walk down the aisle.

If you do choose to follow tradition and pay for all the festivities, you're not alone; it's still a surprisingly popular option. Your daughter should feel very, very lucky (and grateful) for your generosity. Consider this: Will you hand a set amount of money to the couple so they can spend it as they see fit? Or do you want to plan the event and write all the checks? The *only* way to avoid hard feelings is for everyone to acknowledge and be clear about their expectations, since many brides today anticipate having final decision-making power even if you foot the entire bill. If you expect to have the last word, that's fine, but your daughter and her fiancé should have the option to politely reject your contribution if that's not what they want.

Another viable option is the three-way split. After you all finalize a budget together, the couple, the bride's family, and the groom's family equally divide the total cost. This approach works best when all parties are in a similar economic boat. If you're better off than the groom's family, for instance, asking them to kick in as much as you will might be a recipe for in-law disaster. And vice versa.

If you feel strongly about certain aspects of the wedding, offer to contribute dollars and attention to those specific costs. You might want to buy her wedding dress, say, or perhaps there's a particular planning task you know she doesn't enjoy. You still need to be clear about how much you have to give and whether you'll feel insulted if your daughter wants to kick in more than you do.

A communal approach—where everyone chips in what they can afford, donates it to the bride and groom, and the couple decides where it will be best spent—has also become a running favorite. If everyone willingly makes the gift they can afford and cedes control of it to the kids, there really aren't going to be many blowups.

Finally, since many brides and grooms are marrying older and earn enough to take care of more costs, they very well might assume the wedding is their responsibility. If this is the case, and if you had your heart set on throwing your daughter's wedding but she and her fiancé have joined forces to say they don't want you to, try not to feel left out. While this emotion is perfectly natural, keep in mind that from their perspective, planning their wedding themselves is not about shutting you out but about starting their life together. Consider taking the money you stored up for her wedding and surprising them with an offer of a down payment for a new house. That's a gift that will last a lifetime.

CHECKS AND BALANCES

Putting a price tag on such an important event is never trouble-free, but it's vital to put all the wedding pieces together. Before you talk with the kids, you and your husband should decide how much you *want* to devote to this event and make sure you're both on the same page. Perhaps you've already earmarked an exact dollar amount for your daughter's nuptials?

The first sit-down sets the tone for the next months or even year of planning, so it's important to be straightforward. Save the couple the embarrassment of asking you for money by telling them what you'd like to contribute (read on for our projected budget breakdown). Then turn the table over to them, asking them what kind of wedding they're dreaming of and what they hope for. In the end, no matter what you all decide on, make sure you are clear about what strings, if any, are attached to your contribution.

Remember, too, that even deep pockets have limits. Before you announce that you're taking care of it all, familiarize yourself with how much weddings cost these days. On average, they're comparable to a year of private-college tuition. But overall budgets vary widely—in urban areas, projected costs can double or even triple. Of course, much depends on what kind of wedding the couple wants; a big bash is more expensive than a small, intimate party, since the single largest factor in cost is the number of guests.

As a starting point, follow the budget breakdown below, which explains the percentage of the total budget devoted to each aspect of the wedding and notes what areas the bride's side has traditionally paid for. Don't think of it as a set of rules but rather as a guideline to get you, your husband, and your kids talking.

Reception: 50 Percent of the Total Budget

By far the biggest-ticket item, because of the hefty cost of food and drinks. The bride's side traditionally takes care of everything, from the site fee and table rentals to the catering and cake. Multiply the "per person" charge the reception space or catering manager quoted you by the number on your guest list and you'll get a sense of the cost of the style of party you want. Also, find out if the space charges additional usage or maintenance fees.

Attire: 10 Percent of the Total Budget

The bride's side takes care of the wedding gown, veil, accessories, hair and makeup, and trousseau (read: lingerie and honeymoon clothes). The groom and his family cover his tuxedo and trimmings. (Attendants are not included in this breakdown; they pay for their own dresses or suits and shoes.) Budgeting for attire really depends on your daughter and her fashion taste. If she's crazy for couture, you can expect to spend many thousands on a dress. But she might be willing to forgo fancy shoes and accessories. Luckily, there are beautiful gowns in all price ranges.

Photography and Video: 10 Percent of the Total Budget

The bride's side takes care of all wedding photo and video costs. Many couples cite photography as the most important wedding element—for obvious sentimental reasons. Therefore, increasing numbers of brides and grooms are choosing to cover the cost themselves.

Flowers and Décor: 10 Percent of the Total Budget

Traditionally, the bride's side takes care of all the arrangements for the ceremony (including finding a huppah if it's a Jewish wedding) and reception sites, plus purchasing the bouquets and corsages for the bridesmaids and flower girls. The groom's side buys the bouquet and going-away corsage, boutonnieres for the men, and corsages for the mothers and grandmothers. But, honestly, it's much easier for one party to foot the floral bill—divvying it up is awkward and outdated. Be aware, too, that many florists these days design the entire space—adding lanterns, plants, and lighting—which can increase costs.

Music and Entertainment: 10 Percent of the Total Budget

The bride's side pays for all entertainment, including the band or DJ for the reception. Top-rated wedding bands usually charge per musician, so, if money's an object, ask if you can, for example, hire only the nine-piece ensemble instead of the full twelve-piece one—just be certain of which musicians are included in the truncated group. DJs, on average, are significantly less expensive than bands. Music during cocktail hour often incurs an additional charge.

Other Details and the Unexpected: 10 Percent of the Total Budget
The bride's side pays for all invitations and paper products and use of the church or synagogue, as well as fees for the sexton and organist, transportation, tips, taxes, and other miscellaneous costs, while the groom's side takes care of the officiant. Both sides are responsible for their own wedding party gifts and the rings.

Note: It's best to factor into this 10 percent any budget blunders (such as not figuring in tips/gratuities and extra meals for the band and photographer), unforeseen circumstances (the lilacs the bride fell in love with have to be flown in from overseas, or there's a heat wave on the horizon and an extra air-conditioning unit is suggested), and last-minute desires (to-die-for lighting that adds obvious oomph to the room, or extra goodies for the welcome baskets).

PRE- AND POSTWEDDING EXPENSES

Engagement Party
The bride's side pays, and the size of the soiree is really up to you.

Bridal Shower
The maid of honor and bridesmaids generally host this affair; if one of your other daughters is in the wedding, you might need to contribute, but tradition holds that it is not appropriate for the family of the bride to throw a shower (see page 75 for more on showers).

Bridesmaids' Luncheon
The bride hosts and pays for this event, which is her thank-you to you and her bridesmaids (as well as any other key players).

Rehearsal Dinner
Traditionally the groom's side pays, unless everyone is splitting all the costs equally. Find more on this topic in chapter 4.

Honeymoon
Traditionally, the groom's side pays for the honeymoon. But again, with modern postwedding vacations extending into two-week extravaganzas, many newlyweds are taking care of these costs on their own.

CREATIVE COST CUTTERS

No matter how hard you all work to stick to a budget, at some point each of you will desperately want to go over budget (read: when she finds *The Dress* and it's a thousand dollars more than you budgeted for it). Wow her with these secret ways to save:

Cool cocktails. Offer a "menu" of both trendy (for the young crowd) and old-fashioned (for the older generation) cocktails. Think sidecars, apple martinis, cosmopolitans—but make sure all are made with just one or two kinds of alcohol. Caterers usually charge for every open bottle, so by sticking to a few kinds of liquor, you will pay for just one or two partially used bottles instead of ten or fifteen.

Simple place settings. Ask the caterer if you can rent cotton napkins instead of linen, silver-plate dinnerware rather than sterling, or simple wineglasses instead of cut crystal. These are the kinds of details people don't tend to notice. The amount saved per place setting might seem insignificant, but it adds up.

Original escort cards. Escort cards can double as favors. For instance, if she's planning a winter wedding, she could decorate a tree outside the reception hall with hundreds of little star ornaments, each adorned with a guest's name—and tagged with their table number.

Ornate cake. Go all out on the designer cake of her dreams—but don't worry about making it big enough to feed everyone. Save a bundle by hiding sheet cakes of the same flavor in the kitchen to serve guests.

Five-star food. Ask the caterer if they'll serve another event close to the time of your reception. Often, if one requests a similar menu, a caterer will offer a discount, since it costs much less to prepare more of the same food than different meals.

Stunning stationery. Is your little darling in love with letterpress? We are, too, but it can drive the cost of paper goods sky high. Suggest she splurge on the invitations, then create a "logo" (this could be a simple motif of the couple's names) and have it letterpressed onto thank-you notes, menus, and other items. Then she can hand-write (for place cards) or computer-print (for menus or drink cards) the rest of the information.

Favors. She can give just one favor per couple. Simply place the favor between the two dinner plates, tagging it with the couple's names.

WEDDING
PLANNING 101

Now that the wedding planning is underway, you'll start to realize that being the mother of the bride is a tremendous honor with an inherent set of responsibilities. Traditionally, the mother of the bride was in complete control of the wedding. She selected the reception and ceremony sites, handpicked the guest list, designed seating charts, tracked wedding gifts and invitation responses, contacted various vendors, and served as official hostess at the reception. But as time wore on, this stereotypical role slowly evolved. These days, brides (and grooms!) are shouldering a large part of the planning themselves, and they expect veto power no matter who is paying for the wedding.

Now, you might already be in the trenches with your daughter, checking out bands and sampling wedding cakes alongside her. But even if she's the one who is picking the professionals, there are still tons of ways you can help out. If she's hiring the photographer, for instance, you can help to create a must-have family portrait shot list.

Be prepared: Wedding planning can be hard work for MOBs as well as brides. Our best advice? Recruit mother-of-the-bride maids. Being constantly supportive of your daughter is a lot easier when you have someone to lean on yourself, so we suggest you create your own team of attendants—call on close female relatives or friends who aren't involved in the wedding planning. Then, when you feel confused, or just want to obsess about what you're going to wear, you'll always have someone to turn to.

In this chapter, you'll find advice on all your major MOB decisions and duties, in roughly chronological order. Feel free to dip in and out of this chapter and to focus on the areas where you really want to pitch in. You and your daughter will decide how much you'll participate in the planning, but whatever the circumstances, there's one commonality: you'll be called on to perform your most motherly duty, supporting the bride in any way, shape, or form needed. Let her cry on your shoulder—you know, be a mom. Strive to make her feel confident in all her choices, secure in her new marriage, calm, and as if she's the most beautiful woman in the world. It's time for you to step back and see what a good job you've done raising her.

IT'S IN THE DETAILS

RECEPTION PERFECTION

All weddings start with a venue selection. Naturally, something near your home would warm your heart, but remember to be supportive of your daughter's wishes— even if you are paying for the wedding. This doesn't mean you must remain a silent partner; speak up if you know the perfect spot that suits her style or if there are ideas that you're completely opposed to (tented weddings, perhaps?). Offer to accompany her on reception venue visits, since the site will set the mood of the entire day. And this is a decision that needs to be made promptly, given that venues tend to book up at least a year in advance.

You could also volunteer to "pre-scout" some locations. First, arm yourself with information: the couple's desired wedding date, the budget, the look and feel the couple wants for the wedding, the time of day they'd prefer to be married, the estimated number of guests, and, of course, our list of the details that can make or break a wedding (see "Reception Site Rules," following). Then grab one of your mother-of-the-bride maids or your hubby and start inspecting.

You'll probably get a gut feeling as soon as you enter a space, but look a little deeper into the room. Check out the bathrooms—are there enough stalls? Are the cleanliness standards up to par? Is there a coatroom, if you need one? Adequate parking? Ask the caterer if you can change the chairs or bring in your own linens, and find out if venue staff are accustomed to hosting parties. Most important, size up the banquet manager or catering supervisor. This is the person with whom you and your daughter will have most contact (unless you hire a full-time consultant). Can you imagine working with him or her on such a highly emotional event? Finally, bring in your daughter and future son-in-law and wait for them to express their feelings about the place first. Most likely, you'll be in complete harmony. Otherwise, broach your concerns only if you think something could be detrimental to her dream party (for example, there's not enough space for rowdy revelers to dance).

If you live far from the city in which your daughter wants to marry, you might have to browse through spaces via the Internet. The good news is that most hotels and popular wedding sites post photos and extensive details online for you to peruse; if you do your research online, your daughter and her fiancé will probably call on you to fly in and help make the final site decision.

You or your daughter might be struck by a desire to host the wedding in your own home—especially if it's where she grew up. An at-home wedding can be both meaningful and demanding. You might be exhilarated by the idea, but there are a wealth of logistics to mull over first, such as renting portable toilets, hiring a valet, erecting a tent, and bringing in a caterer. Unless you're hosting a very intimate or casual reception, by the time you add up all the required elements, a home reception will probably be more expensive than your local reception hall. Nonetheless, sentimentality and comfort might trump troubles and technicalities.

RECEPTION SITE RULES

Number one, the place needs to have that certain something—charm, personality, depth—that just feels "right." Then, scope out the specifics.

Size it up. Make sure the spot is the right size for your guest list. A space, even an outdoor lawn, might look enormous when it's empty, but wedding essentials—tables, chairs, a buffet, a bar, the band, the dance floor—fill up a room fast. On the other hand, packing in guests just right creates a festive environment that is alive with energy. The best way to assess the size of a site? Ask to check out the place when another wedding is setting up there.

Go with the flow. Think of the wedding as a giant dinner party. There should be logical places within the space where guests can eat, drink, talk, and dance. If a room is too small to separate into sections accordingly, you might feel cramped (especially if your ceremony is held there, too). An S-shaped area or some other oddball configuration could compromise the party's flow as well. Also, note the locations of columns or other obstructions in the room—will they block people's views?

Light it right. If your daughter is marrying during the day, be certain your hall has plenty of windows. Who wants to spend six hours in a dark room when the sun is shining? If she's marrying outdoors—say, at dusk—can you set out candles if necessary? Try to visit the site at the same time of day that the wedding will be held. Even if the space looks swell by candlelight, you could be surprised by the sight of that faded wallpaper during the day.

Match the mood. If your daughter is considering a certain theme and color palette—say, a Midsummer Night's Dream with light green, cream, and gold accents—a red shag carpet could wreck the effect. The site's colors don't have to be perfect, but the walls, carpets, chairs, and curtains shouldn't clash or conflict with the party's mood. If she wants the feeling of a Victorian tea, look for a space that's done in pastel colors or florals; for modern elegance, consider a room decorated in black and white.

Mind your minutes. How long will your guests want to dance? Well, probably all night, but check to see how long you can book the space for, from set-up to cleanup. If it's a daytime celebration, ask if there's an evening party that starts immediately after the event—you don't want to rush the bride. For nighttime weddings, find out when the room closes and if the venue has another space for a lively after-party.

Prevent party crashers. Banquet halls and hotels often hold more than one affair at a time. If other events will be going on simultaneously in rooms close to yours, you might hear karaoke-loving guests singing through the walls or meet them over the hot-air dryers in the bathroom. If this bothers you, schedule the wedding when there won't be another party next door. If this is impossible, visit the site on a dual-party night and see how sound carries and whether there are any major people problems. Don't forget to ask about staffing (the norm is one waiter per ten guests)—will there be enough help to cater to both parties?

Prepare for Mother Nature. If you choose an outdoor site, you need a backup plan. For summer weddings, you could reserve an alternate air-conditioned location nearby in case the temperature flirts with the triple digits. Industrial fans or a mist tent can also cool off a crowd—just make sure your space has the capacity to hold them. Rain won't dampen your spirits (or your party) if you set up an emergency rain tent— a must for spring celebrations. Some even are equipped with heaters for sudden cold spells.

Look for budget breaks. Built-in cost cuts can help lessen the blow, so take stock of your space's resources (also known as money-saving extras!). A bonus for marrying at a botanical garden? A diminished florist bill. If your reception is in a hotel where many guests will stay, you might get a discount for bringing in business. Negotiate! They should throw in perks—such as an upgrade to the honeymoon suite for the newlyweds.

CEREMONY CUES

Who's going to perform the marriage? Deciding between a religious and a civil ceremony is the first issue you need to resolve. Your daughter and her fiancé might already have decided to exchange vows in the house of worship you have always attended, with your family priest or rabbi as officiant. If so, you're lucky. Take the reins and find out if there are any necessary preparations (such as pre-Cana in Catholicism) or any fees, what paperwork is needed (birth certificates, bar mitzvah records), and if there are any special rules (no aisle runners, organs only) to consider.

Or maybe they've decided to hold the ceremony in a separate room at the reception site and to have it performed by a justice of the peace recommended by a friend. If you are okay with a nonreligious wedding, then you're set. Again, take it upon your-self to find out if there are any fees, paperwork, and so on, and speak with the recep-tion site staff about the specific logistics of setting up the ceremony area.

⌜DECIDING ON A DATE⌝

Surely you'll be intimately involved in picking the date—the mother of the bride must be able to attend, of course! Here are some things to keep in mind:

1. Allow enough time for advance planning (a year is standard) so that you will be able to secure your favorite vendors and not rush into any decisions. A wedding can be planned in less time, of course, but it won't be as relaxing.

2. Avoid other family members' or close family friends' weddings by at least two weeks. You don't want anyone to have to cut her honeymoon short.

3. It's best to choose two potential dates. If you are particular about key elements (your preferred officiant, having it at the club), flexibility could help.

4. Holiday weekends offer pros and cons. There is an extra day for the festivities (and recovery!), and you might be able to host the affair on Sunday, which often costs less than a Saturday event. However, costs of travel and hotels might increase. Also, some families have standing holiday weekend plans or traditions.

5. Religious holidays or historically significant days can cause a conflict for some guests.

6. Choosing a popular wedding month, such as May, June, September, or October, could limit your choice of venues and vendors.

7. Check to see if any special events will be going on in the prospective city or town. A large conference or expo could fill hotels and venues.

8. Consider pregnant family members' due dates.

9. When you do decide on a date, start spreading the word among key friends and family so they don't inadvertently plan their own daughter's wedding— or other important events—on your date.

However, it might not be this easy. Religious clashes between generations are not uncommon, and you cannot expect your daughter to follow your faith just because it means a lot to you. If you want a religious wedding, speak with her about her beliefs and why she prefers a civil ceremony. If the groom is of a different faith, a civil marriage might make most sense for them. Support her at all costs, and don't let religion interfere with your relationship. This is not the time to express disapproval of their ceremony ideas—your daughter might pull away from you. In the end, keep in mind that she'll still be a radiant bride wherever she says her "I dos."

If your daughter is marrying into another culture or religion, a great way to show your support is to do some research—become acquainted with (if not educated on) the key rituals of his religion. If it feels comfortable, you could even call your counterpart, the mother of the groom, and ask her for the basics.

Now, *your* mother or father might not be as open-minded. If Grandmother (or Grandfather) expresses disdain for the civil setting or the interfaith ceremony, firmly explain that it is your daughter's wedding and that these are her wishes. And don't try to blame it on the bride and groom; they are probably having a hard enough time already. If she refuses to accept it, gently suggest that she not attend the ceremony if it makes her uncomfortable. She'll likely come around in the end.

PHOTOGRAPHY POINTERS

The photographer is arguably the most important professional your daughter will hire, since he or she is the one who will ensure the day lives beyond everyone's memories. When your mom planned your wedding, she probably made just one call to the portrait photographer *everyone* used. But given today's broader range of photography styles and advances in technology, your daughter has a lot more options.

The main question she'll consider is what photography style best suits her and her fiancé. Don't gasp when she says she wants only candid shots taken by a photojournalist (a photographer who prefers a documentary-style, unposed feeling in pictures). Any wedding photographer will still take formal family portraits—if you establish a plan ahead of time. A great time to take your family and bridal-party pictures is before the ceremony, when the bride is fully dressed and everyone's excited and fresh. Then, between the ceremony and reception, schedule time for the full family portraits (yours and the in-laws') as well.

Create a list of the formal portraits you want the photographer to reserve time for: the bride and her parents; the bride, her parents, and her siblings; you and the bride; your husband and the bride; just the siblings; Mom helping the bride with her veil. You get the idea. The list enables the photographer to estimate how long the roundup of formal photos will require, so you can plan your day accordingly.

Earn some brownie points with your daughter—suggest she include a few more interesting shots as well. Your daughter probably has thumbed through your wedding album more times than you can count, and likely has her own favorite photo: perhaps Grandpa with his pockets turned inside out or her dad smooching your cheek. Suggest that your daughter and her fiancé re-create each of their favorite shots from their respective parents' wedding albums . . . we guarantee they won't be the only ones to treasure them! Or propose that the photographer get a shot of her walking off with her honey, hand in hand, into the sunset. She might dismiss this as corny, but if the photographer shoots them moving away and at a distance, with lots of sky in the background, they will have the perfect shot to end their album— we promise!

Your radar might go up when you hear that your daughter's considering a photographer who shoots digitally. If so, know that today's professional digital cameras are incredibly advanced and take crystal-clear pictures, and digital photos are processed faster and offer more convenient distribution options (such as viewing images online) than conventional photos. In fact, an increasing number of wedding photographers, including some of the industry's best, now shoot digitally. One caveat: The couple should make sure the photographer will use the latest equipment, since only the most advanced professional digital cameras yield prints that are as good as standard thirty-five-millimeter prints.

WORKING WITH VENDORS

If you hold the purse strings, it's particularly important that you take the hiring of professionals and signing contracts seriously. Here are some pointers:

1. Head online and scope out potential professionals for each element of the wedding. The Knot (www.theknot.com) offers a wealth of vendor leads and reviews.

2. Always ask for a written proposal with an estimate. You don't want to return to hire a vendor and be shocked by a different price quote.

3. Call the references provided—or ask friends or other wedding professionals if they've heard of a particular vendor.

4. Avoid hiring someone who isn't familiar with your site. You should visit the site with the vendor so he can learn the necessary set-up rules and precautions.

5. Clarify which costs are included in the fee, such as a weighty travel charge.

6. Finally, read over the contract with a magnifying glass. It might list demands that you are not prepared for, such as meal requests or an abundance of break times. You want to make sure everyone is on the same page.

SELECTING THE SOUNDS

Your daughter has visions of boogying the night away to hip-hop favorites, while you would love to see an Ol' Blue Eyes clone take the stage with slower songs. Music tastes are so generational and weddings so multigenerational, it's no wonder booking a band can be tricky. But no matter what kind of music your daughter and her fiancé favor, there are ways to ensure everyone will be happy.

First, you and your daughter should tailor the music to the space's acoustic conditions. A jazz combo sounds better at an intimate art gallery than a fourteen-piece orchestra does. Check out the room's sound quality during an event—if the place is too echoey, it could give weird reverb to the music, not to mention make it difficult for guests to hear one another talking. A tile or wood floor, for example, amplifies sounds, while a thick carpet tends to muffle them. Cruise around the room to see if it has enough power outlets for the entertainers.

Once the band (or DJ) is booked, ask your daughter to print you a copy of the band's song list. That way, you can highlight tunes that you really want to hear and make sure the band or DJ will play songs that span several decades, from Duke Ellington and Motown to the latest dance hits. Ask if they can kick off the night with intergenerational songs everyone will enjoy: those by the Beatles, Sinatra, or Patsy Cline, for example.

As the evening progresses and curfew-bound relatives start to say adieu, let the band bust out the couple's favorite age-appropriate tunes. The older set probably is gearing up to leave anyway.

FATHER-DAUGHTER DANCE TRACKS

It's safe to assume your daughter's got her own ideas about what song she'll use for her first dance with her new husband, but she'll likely welcome any and all suggestions when it comes time for her to take the floor with her daddy.

"A Song for My Daughter" (Ray Allaire)
"Brown Eyed Girl" (Van Morrison)
"Daddy's Girl" (Peter Cetera)
"Daddy's Hands" (Holly Dunn)
"Daddy's Little Girl" (Al Martino)
"Have I Told You Lately" (Van Morrison or Rod Stewart)
"Hero" (Mariah Carey)
"I Believe in Miracles" (Engelbert Humperdinck)
"If I Could" (Ray Charles)
"In My Life" (The Beatles)
"Isn't She Lovely" (Stevie Wonder)
"Just the Way You Are" (Billy Joel)
"Lean on Me" (Bill Withers)
"Lullabye (Goodnight My Angel)" (Billy Joel)
"My Girl" (The Temptations)
"She's Leaving Home" (The Beatles)
"Thank Heaven for Little Girls" (Merle Haggard)
"Through the Years" (Kenny Rogers)
"Times of Your Life" (Paul Anka)
"Turn Around" (Harry Belafonte)
"Unforgettable" (Nat King Cole/Natalie Cole)
"Way You Look Tonight" (Frank Sinatra)
"What a Wonderful World" (Louis Armstrong)
"You Are the Sunshine of My Life" (Stevie Wonder)
"Your Smiling Face" (James Taylor)

There are no longer any strict rules on wedding-appropriate flowers. So whether your daughter wants tulips in winter, loves the look of fruits mixed with flowers, or has her heart set on elaborate arrangements she found in a photo, she can probably pull it off. Literally, the only thing stopping her will be the budget. And you should be prepared for the floral estimate to be higher than you imagined, given the labor involved, the high cost of bulk flowers, and the intricate delivery and installation required. It's the one cost that most often surprises people.

KEEPING DADDY BUSY

Just as grooms are taking a more active role these days, so, too, are many fathers of the bride. If your husband wants to be part of the planning but just doesn't know where to pitch in, suggest he do the following:

- Create a multigenerational list of dance tunes, noting his all-time favorite songs and canvassing the older folks for theirs.

- Prepare a toast—or work with you on shared remarks.

- Research honeymoon options and travel deals.

- Arrange guests' transportation to and from the wedding festivities.

- Make maps with directions to the wedding site(s) to include in invitations.

- Work with the caterer on the wine list.

- Present a few choices for the father-daughter dance.

- Scout reliable tux rental shops.

- Stay until the celebration's bitter end and settle the final bills for the couple.

If your precious girl is getting married in winter but desperately wants to plaster the place with peonies (that was the first flower her fiancé ever sent her!), they'll need to be imported from as far away as New Zealand, but this is no place to cut corners. But if it's just the *look* of peonies she loves, suggest she try big bouquets of full open roses, which can look similar but almost always cost less than her chosen flower. In fact, if she's trying to re-create any style found in a photo, she might start by asking the florist to achieve the "look" rather than to reproduce the arrangements. Most florists are savvy about coming up with in-season alternatives, which means less hassle—and certainly less expense—in getting the flowers.

It's tradition that the mothers of the bride and groom, grandmothers, and special aunts are adorned with honorary flowers. Whether they'll carry a nosegay (a small bouquet, approximately six to eight inches in diameter, composed of densely packed flowers, greenery, and occasionally herbs) or wear a corsage, talk to your daughter about ideas she has for the blooms. You and the groom's mom and grandmothers, as well as other important female relatives, should all sport similar arrangements.

SAVE-THE-DATE AND INVITE ESSENTIALS

Save-the-date cards are a heads-up about the wedding and are sent approximately six months before the event and four months before the actual invitations go out. They are a must for destination weddings to which most guests must travel, for weddings scheduled during a holiday weekend or high season (such as summertime in a beach town), and for weddings where accommodations must be reserved many months ahead of time. Typically, save-the-dates list the wedding date, location, and suggested lodging. For weddings in faraway lands, send them earlier (eight to ten months before the date) to allow time for plane-ticket purchases.

Start looking at invitations and order the save-the-dates when you've settled on an overall look. The actual invitations should be sent eight weeks before the wedding. Allow ample time for printing both items, as processes such as letterpress can require several weeks if you're ordering a large number.

Consider all the pieces of the invitation: the reply card (to determine whose address should be used, see "RSVP Requisites" on page 48) and additional inserts (do you want to spend more to include directions and accommodations listings?). Your daughter probably will narrow down a list of lovely paper options, but she will likely bring you into the conversation if the invitations will list you and your husband as the hosts. As the mom, you'll want to make sure the style and wording suit the event's formality level.

⌈ SAY IT OUT LOUD ⌉

Here are four examples of invitation wordings:

THE TRADITIONAL, PART I

 Mr. and Mrs. John Doe
 request the honor of your presence
 at the marriage of their daughter
 Jane Doe
 to
 Charles Smith

**THE TRADITIONAL, PART II
(INCLUDING THE IN-LAWS)**

 Mr. and Mrs. John Doe
 request the honor of your presence
 at the marriage of their daughter
 Jane Doe
 to
 Charles Smith
 son of Mr. and Mrs. William Smith

THE PROGRESSIVE COUPLE

 Ms. Jane Doe and Mr. Charles Smith
 request the honor of your presence
 at their marriage . . .

THE EGALITARIAN APPROACH

 Ms. Jane Doe and Mr. Charles Smith
 together with their parents [names optional]
 request the honor of your presence . . .

RSVP REQUISITES

The traditional MOB role of RSVP manager might be a good one for you to embrace. Not only will it be a huge help to your daughter, but it will give you an opportunity to become familiar with all the guests. We're sure the bride will be ever so grateful for a top-line summary of who's coming—especially when the reply date comes and goes and fifty responses are still missing.

If you decide to take on the task, make sure your mailing address is printed on the reply cards (otherwise, it should be your daughter's home address). It's also essential to create a spreadsheet or use an online guest manager to track the responses. Spreadsheets make it easier to sort replies and figure out the final head count than does the good old-fashioned method of collecting RSVPs into shoeboxes. If you're not computer-savvy, ask your daughter or future son-in-law (good bonding points) for a quick tutoring session. Strange as it might sound, some people actually forget to write their names on the reply card. Be prepared for such a bind by assigning every invited guest or couple a number on your spreadsheet, and lightly pencil it in the lower right-hand corner of the back of each reply card. That way, if someone forgets to include his name or you can't decode his handwriting, you'll have a cheat sheet to check.

Brides and grooms often leave space on the reply card for guests to write a senti-mental note or good wishes; consider purchasing a scrapbook to showcase these words of congratulations. However, some guests also use the reply card as an oppor-tunity to add an uninvited friend or significant other to your guest list. Before you stress out your daughter, tackle the issue yourself. If a family member or friend of yours tries to bring along an extra guest, simply call the etiquette offender and explain that you can allow only a certain number of guests at the reception. It could be an honest mistake. A nice way to soften the blow is to say that you'll keep the name on your list in case extra spaces open up once all the RSVPs have come in, but stress that you will call back if it's possible. If it is one of your daughter's friends or someone from the in-laws' list, consider sharing the news and asking them to make the call. After all, they might have a better idea of the extenuating circumstances.

If the RSVP deadline has passed without all replies, don't feel awkward about picking up the phone and calling guests—it's perfectly acceptable and necessary. The invitation might have been lost in the mail or the invitee might have recently moved. Send out a replacement right away, and make a note of the guests' decision—at this point (approximately one month before the wedding), they should know whether they will be able to attend.

SETTLING ON SEATING

Once the reply cards finally all pour in and the head count is set (about two weeks before the big day), you and your daughter should tackle the ultimate people puzzle—the seating chart. Even if your daughter determines where her friends will sit, it's a good idea to create your own chart. After all, you know best which of your friends and relatives can or can't sit next to each other.

Obviously, if it's a really intimate affair—we're talking fifty or fewer people—assigned seating might not be necessary. But with any number over that, ensure that you carefully arrange how the party sits. People like to know where they will sit— and avoid the chaos of trying to secure a great table with a great group of people on the fly—and your caterer might need to know where people who need special meals will sit. A seating chart is also a great way to keep family tensions and hostilities at bay.

A new spreadsheet can be your biggest ally here. If you haven't already done so, insert a column into your guest-list document that categorizes all the invitees by relationship: bride's friend; bride's family; groom's friend; groom's family; bride's family friend; groom's family friend. This way, you can simply sort the list and break it down into logical table assortments. Now separate these lists into distinct tables. You can either create a new column in your spreadsheet for table numbers or go low-tech and write every guest's name on a Post-It to arrange in mock table patterns on a piece of poster board.

Place the key figures first. The traditional "head table" on a dais is long and straight and generally faces all the other reception tables. Usually the bride and groom sit smack-dab in the middle of the head table (where everyone can see them), with the maid of honor next to the groom, the best man next to the bride, and then the rest of the party boy-girl from there. Flower girls or ringbearers usually sit at the tables where their parents sit. Or encourage your daughter to think about a more modern head table: the couple sits at a round table with their parents and siblings. She might even opt for a sweetheart table for two. In that case, traditionally you and the groom's parents would all sit at another table, along with grandparents, siblings not in the wedding party, and the officiant and his/her spouse, if they attend the reception. If you would rather not sit with the in-laws, each set of parents could host their own table. Or if you are divorced, you and your ex could each host your own table. This might make things easier on everyone.

Ask your daughter if she would prefer mixing up groups or keeping those with common bonds together. For the most part, seating good friends together makes for a more enjoyable dinner for many guests. Of course, there might also be certain family members who just do *not* get along. Maybe they haven't spoken in years. Understandably, you want to keep them as far apart as possible. Think about these relationships (or lack thereof) before you even begin making your chart so you can take them into consideration from the start. Let your daughter handle the younger generations—she likely knows best who will do well with whom. And perhaps she'll make a few matches in the process.

ENTERTAINING OUT-OF-TOWNERS

Greeting and caring for your guests are crucial parts of any wedding. This isn't a time for just the bride and groom—otherwise, why invite anyone in the first place? If busloads of out-of-towners are coming to the wedding, you and your daughter need to figure out where they'll sleep, how they'll get around, and what they'll do in their spare time. Pitch in with the guest planning to give your bride a break.

First, figure out who will pay for guests' trips. These days, usually people pay their own way. If some family members simply can't afford to pay their way, consider covering one night of their hotel bill.

About six to eight months before the big day, contact a local hotel convenient to your wedding site to ask about discounted group rates should you send all your guests their way. Reserve a block of rooms, then be sure to spread the word. Be considerate of travelers' budgets; you might offer several options in varying price ranges. If the wedding is near your home, be wary of inviting guests—even intimate family members—to stay there. It will be a hectic forty-eight hours leading up to the main event, and you don't want to worry about entertaining in your own home.

Provide maps and directions ahead of time for those renting cars—or you can welcome them in style by arranging a pick-up at the airport. This task could involve finding out flight arrival times and gates, booking limos, and asking helpful relatives or friends to provide shuttle services. Coordinating everyone's transportation can be tricky, so make sure you're organized and have all the information at hand. Create a transportation team (maybe the best man and the father of the groom?), and assign helpers.

Show your love for guests by asking the hotel to place welcome baskets in their hotel rooms. Fill them with fruit, local gourmet specialties, bottled water, and a packet of information including the weekend's itinerary, maps of the area, and things to do.

⌈ P L A Y I N G   F A V O R I T E S ⌉

Not so long ago, brides gave their departing guests a container of Jordan almonds and called it a day. Nowadays, favors are thought of as a final chance to make a lasting impression. Here's a list of our favorites:

- Send guests home with mini-wine bottles of the same vintage served at the wedding dinner, adorned with a personalized label.

- Is she marrying around the winter holidays? Give Christmas ornaments in ivory, silver, or gold, tied with a velvet ribbon stenciled with the bride's and groom's names and wedding date.

- For guests attending a winter wedding, slip a frosted snowflake cookie into a glassine bag tied with white satin ribbon.

- Package a collection of family recipes in a small box with the couple's names and wedding date printed on its back.

- Hometown goods, such as locally baked cookies, maple syrup, candies, or anything sweet made in the city where the couple weds, always make memorable favors.

- For DIY favors, hand out Chinese take-out boxes stamped with the bridal couple's new monogram, and let guests fill them up with sugary sweets of their choice from a penny candy cart.

- With artfully decorated jars of jam, you can "spread the love" to family and friends.

- For a beach bash, give each guest a pair of flip-flops (ask for each person's shoe size on the reply card).

- "Mint to Be Together" labels on breathsavers will inspire some smooches.

- Fill tiny terra-cotta pots with lavender or another favorite herb. Secure nametags to the pots, and the favors can double as place cards.

- Fill a basket with individual packets of seeds, such as forget-me-nots or your favorite bloom. On the outside, attach a thank-you note, the couple's wedding vows, or the lyrics to their first dance song.

- Paper folding fans in floral patterns keep guests cool during the ceremony and are easy to slip into one's purse or pocket on the way out.

- Small silver picture frames engraved with the wedding date can double as place-card holders.

- Leave notes at each place setting explaining that a donation has been made in guests' names to a favorite charity.

- Burn CDs of the wedding day music or favorite tunes and slip them into a personalized CD cover.

- Give guests astrological-reading scrolls tied with sheer ribbon (ask everyone to write his or her birth date on the RSVP cards).

- For an Easter occasion, place handmade Easter eggs, dipped in decorative colors, in mini–Easter baskets filled with raffia instead of green plastic grass.

- Crowd an entire table with miniature watering cans full of fresh spring blooms.

- Add a handful of Swedish fish or saltwater taffy to tiny tin pails adorned with a sand-dollar or starfish magnet for a summer wedding on the water.

FINAL PLANNING POINTERS

LAST-MINUTE TO-DOS

Your daughter will probably need her mom, the ultimate caregiver, most in the final week before the wedding, so you'll want to be there to help tame tensions. There's so much to consider when planning a wedding that the bride can often feel that she's bound to forget something. Plus, it's a nice way to take some wedding day stress off your daughter. Here's what should be on your list of things for you or someone else (a day-of coordinator, perhaps?) to accomplish in the week before the wedding:

❑ Give the officiant the rehearsal details and the wedding day schedule.

❑ Confirm delivery locations, times, and arrangement count with the florist.

❑ Confirm all final payment amounts with your vendors.

❑ Confirm location, date, and time with the photographer, videographer, and cake baker, as well as the band, DJ, and/or ceremony or cocktail musicians.

❑ Confirm all lodging and transportation for attendants, family, and out-of-towners.

❑ Give the seating chart and favors to the caterer, location manager, or host.

❑ Prepare your toast if necessary (see our tips in chapter 5).

❑ Fax transportation providers a schedule and addresses for pick-ups.

❑ Distribute wedding day directions, schedule, and contact list to all vendors.

❑ Designate who will meet, greet, and handle each vendor on the wedding day.

- Put final payments and cash tips in marked envelopes to distribute on the wedding day—even if you're not paying. (Good job for Dad!)

- Pick up the wedding gown and veil.

- If the bride will dress in your home, clean up and make the area presentable.

- Confirm big-day beauty appointments.

- Make sure the groom (and his attendants!) get haircuts.

- Designate someone (maybe you?) to collect the wedding gifts (and any cash) brought to the reception.

- Confirm the bride and groom's wedding night accommodations.

- Deliver welcome baskets to hotels and arrange for them to be placed in rooms.

MOTHER-OF-THE-BRIDE BEAUTY

THE WEDDING STUDIO
BY ANNA GRIFFIN

INVITATION PRINTING INSTRUCTIONS

1. Open your word processing software.
2. Adjust your document size to match your invitation: 5.25" x 7.75" for cardstock invitations, 4.5" x 7" for vellum overlay invitations (Item Nos. WS301, WS302 and WS303); or, 4.75" x 6.75" for your response card. Set all document margins as indicated on your Test Sheet.
3. Select a font and type your wording. Adjust the font and size as desired. (See wording and layout samples on the reverse of this sheet). Run spell check.
4. Preview your invitation or response card with the print preview option.
5. Place the enclosed Test Sheet in the manual feed tray on your printer.
6. Print one copy on the enclosed Test Sheet to verify that the wording is positioned correctly. Make any necessary revisions or changes.
7. Print your invitations, assemble and mail.

INVITATION ASSEMBLY INSTRUCTIONS

For gatefold vellum invitations (Item Nos. WS401, WS402 and WS403): Place the printed, cardstock invitation inside the folded vellum sheet. Wrap a length of ribbon around the vellum and tie in the front with a bow.

For vellum overlay invitations (Item Nos. WS301, WS302 and WS303): Place the printed, vellum invitation on top of a patterned cardstock sheet, carefully aligning the holes at top. Insert each end of a length of ribbon through one of the holes. From the back side, take the right streamer and thread up through the left hole. Now, take the left streamer and thread up through the right hole. Pull the ends taught and trim any excess.

The invitations and response cards are inserted into the large envelope in size order with the invitation first. Next, the response envelope is placed face down on top of the invitation, with the response card facing up, under its flap.

Wedding invitations should be mailed 4-6 weeks prior to the wedding. Invitations usually incur extra postage because of their weight. Prior to mailing, take the finished invitations to the Post Office and weigh to determine postage.

Add a finishing touch to your event by using the coordinating place cards, thank you notes, programs, guest books and stickers/seals.

THE WEDDING STUDIO
BY ANNA GRIFFIN

INVITATION WORDING AND LAYOUT

Traditionally, wedding invitations are printed in black ink, with centered type in a formal font. They are always phrased in the third person. "Request the honour of your presence" is used when the wedding ceremony is held in a house of worship. The English spelling of "honour" is commonly used. For all other locations use "request the pleasure of your company." You can follow the wording samples shown below, or use them as a starting point for your own creation!

Given by the Bride's Parents

Mr. and Mrs. Robert Wesley Thomas
request the honour of your presence
at the marriage of their daughter
Gwendolyn Merritt
to
Mr. William Garret Barnes
Saturday, the fifteenth of May
Two thousand four
at six o'clock
First Baptist Church
125 Main Street
Dallas, Texas

Given by Both Parents

Together with their parents
Miss Gwendolyn Merritt Thomas
and
Mr. William Garret Barnes
request the honour of your presence
at their marriage
Saturday, the fifteenth of May
Two thousand four
at six o'clock
First Baptist Church
125 Main Street
Dallas, Texas

Given by the Bride & Groom

The honour of your presence
is requested at the marriage of
Miss Gwendolyn Merritt Thomas
to
Mr. William Garret Barnes
Saturday, the fifteenth of May
Two thousand four
at six o'clock
First Baptist Church
125 Main Street
Dallas, Texas

Wedding Announcement

Mr. and Mrs. Robert Wesley Thomas
have the honour of announcing
the marriage of their daughter
Gwendolyn Merritt
to
Mr. William Garret Barnes
Saturday, the fifteenth of May
Two thousand four
at six o'clock
First Baptist Church
125 Main Street
Dallas, Texas

Response or Reception Card

The favour of a reply
is requested before the tenth of April

M_____

will _____ attend

Reception
immediately following ceremony
Cross Creek Country Club

M _____

will _____ attend

Reception
at seven o'clock in the evening
301 West Pine Drive

As essential as it is for the bride to look incredible on the big day, you need to look just as fetching. After all, this is your big moment, too, and you want your daughter to show off dear young Mom! Here we show you how to pull together the quintessential mother-of-the-bride look—polished, calm, confident, and classy—and help you figure out what it takes to feel fabulous. One: A dress that makes you feel tall, slim, and fashionable yet is perfectly appropriate for Mom. Two: A color that flatters and coordinates with the wedding while remaining in tune with the season. Three: Accessories that add polish, shoes that are comfortable, and jewels that dazzle. Four: Make-up that brings out your real beauty. Five: Being comfortable in your skin: this will help you shine all wedding day long.

In this chapter, we take you on a fantasy shopping trip, moving from fabric tips and color choices based on the wedding style to shapes that flatter your figure. We give you all the resources you need to maximize your dressing-room time and minimize your waistline. And we can't forget your big-day beauty routine; we help you put your best face forward so you'll light up that camera lens. Get ready to get gorgeous!

WHAT TO WEAR

DECIDING ON A WEDDING DAY LOOK

Unless you're a charity ball regular, it's safe to say you haven't looked for a dress this important since you searched for your own wedding gown. Mother-of-the-bride dresses are a special breed. You want something that's absolutely fabulous and flattering, but your search is limited by the wedding's overall dress code. Before you start flipping through the dress racks (at the six- to eight-months-before-the-day mark), spend a little time thinking about wedding logistics. Just as with your daughter's gown, the time, setting, and season of the event dictate appropriate attire for you. The mother of the bride can get away with dressing up a notch, but donning a sequined ball gown for a champagne brunch will make you feel out of place. And nothing helps you radiate more than feeling calm, confident, and comfortable on the wedding day. Here are the overarching factors to consider.

The Time and Season

Daytime weddings and evening affairs have their own explicit sets of dress codes. For the day, keep your fabrics light and colors bright. In the evening, it's more acceptable to flaunt beads, sequins, and other sparkles in darker hues. Similarly, hemlines get shorter as the summer days get longer (one exception: floor-length is always fitting for a black-tie affair). And fabrics and colors change with the seasons: bold colors and airy fabrics lighten the warmer months, while deeper tones and rich materials warm up the fall and winter.

The Location

Where will the ceremony and reception take place? A ballroom? A park? A vineyard? If you'll be outdoors at a botanical garden in the early morning, for instance, you'll want to forgo a gown that skims the dewy ground. Or, if the wedding is outdoors, will you need to trek through a garden? Will there be air-conditioning in summer or a good heating system in winter? Will you need to do a lot of walking or sitting? You get the idea. Which style of dress normally makes you feel most comfortable? Remember, you might be wearing this one from early morning until late at night.

Your Daughter's Desires

Chances are, your daughter has a few ideas about what she'd like you to wear on her wedding day—brides don't like big surprises, and we're guessing you don't either. So take her shopping with you; plan a fun day around it.

First, talk about what she's wearing—if she will walk down the aisle in a strapless sheath, look for a tank-style dress or something with light sleeves. Then ask for her "what not to wear" list: Are there certain colors to steer clear of (besides white, of course)? She might be adverse to anything too bright or flashy. Does she think a V-neckline is too revealing? Is she afraid you'll clash with her color scheme?

Then insist that the bride offer you her ideas, which will save you valuable shopping time. Explain your issues, if any (a certain color doesn't look good on you, perhaps, or she's thinking about a style that you feel just won't suit you), and see if you can find common ground. Black is totally acceptable for a mother to wear nowadays, and it goes with any color and just about any type of event.

If you disagree with the dress your daughter has in mind, don't argue—just try on everything, and one of two things will happen. One, she'll see why you don't like a particular dress shape, or, two, you'll fall in love with something that you didn't think you'd like. Either way, you should shop with her so that even if she *says* she doesn't care what you wear, she's there to help guide your decision. Or maybe she knows what great taste you have and trusts you completely—that's how it should be.

The Mother of the Groom's Look

Compare notes with the groom's mom—you'll both feel more comfortable if your elegance is in sync. If you follow tradition, the mother of the bride should be allowed the first opportunity to choose a dress so you won't end up with the same one. However, you might be confronted with a MOG who isn't up on her etiquette. Either way, just opening up a line of communication probably will make things easier for both parties. After all, she's probably as anxious about the purchase as you are.

Call her a few days before you go shopping. Say, "I'm heading out to get my dress for the wedding this weekend. I'll let you know how it goes and what color I end up getting. Any suggestions as to where I should look?" This accomplishes a few things. First, you let her know you're going shopping, and, second, she'll let *you* know where she likes to shop, so you can avoid getting the same dress.

Don't flip out if she's not on board with the rules—she might have budget constraints or limited retail options. She might already own a fabulous evening gown in navy blue. In that case, just go out and buy your own gown, and don't worry about coordinating the effort. Bottom line: A matching level of formality is key (a sundress and sequins at either end of the group wedding photo would look a little off), but harmonizing the colors is not so critical.

Worried about your guests following these norms, too? One of the best ways to let everyone in on the formality of the wedding is via the invitations. If you're hosting a black-tie affair, you can say so plainly on the front of the invitation. Likewise, if the country club requires jackets, include that fact at the bottom of the invitation.

SEASON-BY-SEASON STYLE

Find the perfect gown based on the wedding's style and season.

STYLE	SPRING	SUMMER	FALL	WINTER
Semiformal	A pastel-colored cotton-blend skirt suit will, uh, suit a casual spring celebration.	We promise you won't look like a bride-to-be in a cream-colored linen suit. Just comfortable.	Pair a long-sleeved wool dress in a fun fall color (plum, marigold, or rust) with a bolero.	A plain navy or black velvet cocktail dress with your grand-mother's hand-crocheted shawl will keep you perfectly elegant for the season.
Formal	A lightweight cocktail dress in a hue that's a variation on the wedding colors will perfectly match the day.	Find a fun, flirty, floor-length chiffon number in a bright color such as aqua or salmon.	Flaunt your gams with a two-piece knee-length ensemble in an earthy tone such as olive green or pumpkin that also boasts a fabulous lacy or beaded bodice.	A black pantsuit in a very formal fabric such as satin, paired with a fabulous beaded top and an elegant pair of shoes, has total dazzling power.
Black tie	Silk shantung is supremely formal but not too heavy for the season. Pick an evening gown in a cool shade: think pink, perhaps?	Keep your cool in a strapless, floor-length lace or silk organza gown in a rich color such as navy blue or emerald green.	Try taffeta in rich chocolate-brown, burnt sienna, or eggplant tones. Sequins and beads will put a little sparkle into the season.	Stand out in a sea of black-tie beauties by airing a black or burgundy duchesse satin or velvet evening gown with a gorgeous fur wrap.

FINDING THE PERFECT DRESS

YOUR FIGURE

Now that you've decided on the style, you need to make that all-important dress decision: What looks good on you? It can seem daunting, especially if you're not 100 percent happy with your body type. But, contrary to what you might think, the gorgeous fabrics and styles of formal gowns are actually perfect for hiding a multitude of sins—and showing off your most fabulous features. Here's a quick run-down of common figure flaws and tips on gowns that will camouflage them.

Pear-Shaped

If your bottom half is bigger than your top half, it's best to draw the eye upward. So even if you've never before bared your shoulders, now's the time to consider going strapless, since these dresses are practically made for you. A beautiful strapless ball gown, for instance, broadens your shoulders and balances your entire body. If you're not ready to go quite so bare, a jacket, wrap, or any gown with a show-stopping neckline will do the trick.

Super-Slim

They say you can never be too thin, but you might have a different opinion if you've battled pointy collarbones and a bony pelvis all your life. The right fabrics can add fullness—just skip dresses made of too-clingy silk crepes in favor of those in stiffer, lustrous shantung or dupioni, or anything with layers of lovely chiffon or organza. Just be sure the style you choose shows off those slender arms and ankles!

Broad

If you have a strong swimmer's back, wide shoulders, or a really great set of muscular arms, look for a dress that narrows your top half (a V neck will work beautifully) but shows off your assets at the same time. A dress with a low-cut V-back can also show off your muscular back without broadening you as a barer back might.

Boxy

Or do you consider your figure a boxy one? No hips? No waist? No problem. Again, fuller fabrics—along with the right cut—can *give* you that shapely silhouette you've always wanted. And dresses that have a built-in structure (such as a corset) will lend you the illusion of a bust and waist.

Busty

Nothing shows a well-endowed bustline to better advantage than a beautiful formal gown, and many have built-in bras or corsets. If you dare to bare, find a neckline that frames your chest; if you prefer to cover up, choose a higher-cut bodice. But remember, boat necks and jewel necks can make a big bust appear even bigger—so a V- or scoop neck might be the next best choices. Pair a flattering, closer-fitting top with a fuller skirt.

Plus-Sized

A wedding is one of the few events where one can get by with a full skirt—a cut that actually minimizes full bottoms instead of drawing attention to them. Just be sure to steer clear of bulky pleats, which can add unnecessary weight, and short sleeves, which cut off arms at their widest point.

Hourglass Figure

You have a voluptuous chest, shapely hips, and a tiny waist? Pick out sashes, ribbons, or belts, all of which draw attention to your midsection.

Petite

Conversely, if you're petite, elongate your frame by sticking to dresses that are streamlined and simple and don't cut you off at the waist. Stay away from the thicker, fuller shantung and tulles, which are a bit too bulky for you.

Tall

Ladies with height often have one of two issues—either really long torsos with average legs, or really long legs with short torsos. Choose your dress proportions accordingly. The former should stick to a natural-waist gown (to shorten), while the latter would do well with a dropped waist (to lengthen).

10 WAYS TO LOOK 10 POUNDS THINNER

1. Slim down instantly in a tailored sheath dress. The better the construction, the slimmer the look.

2. Look for gowns with a dropped waist to lengthen the body and slim the figure.

3. If you've fought a belly since you gave birth to your bride-to-be, look for a dress with draping. Ruched and gathered fabric draws the eye in the direction of the drape.

4. Create the illusion of longer, thinner legs with high heels.

5. Draw the eye down from a top-heavy shape with a darker top and brighter bottom. Think: black-and-white gowns, or two-piece ensembles.

6. Cap sleeves and off-the-shoulder dresses take attention off your arms and onto your exposed neck.

7. Wear a suit rather than a dress. The more lines and seams you have, the more ways to camouflage your trouble spots.

8. Minimize your butt with a lightly flared skirt.

9. Horizontal stripes create width; diagonal stripes give a fluid look. And the skinnier the stripe, the thinner you will appear.

10. When all else fails, fade to black.

SHOP TILL YOU DROP

So you've got a good handle on what kind of dress you want and are ready to hit the racks? Even if you're a savvy shopper, it's not always simple to find a mother-of-the-bride dress. But between department stores, which offer a vast selection, and dress-makers, who can fit you to a T, you *will* find something spectacular. Here's what you need to know before you start touring the stores.

Typically, independently owned full-service bridal shops offer the complete roster of services at a range of prices for the entire wedding party, including the mother of the bride. In addition, most bridal shops likely have all the other accessories you need, such as shoes, undergarments, and even jewelry. While an off-the-rack purchase might be available here, this sort of merchant is more likely to offer samples for you to try on or books to thumb through; then the shop will order you a brand-new gown. Price ranges and designers often vary from moderate to high-end, and an owner is usually on the premises, as well as an in-store seamstress who can consult on custom alterations. Try to go during the week, as Saturdays are generally busy with brides. You need to start this process early; stay on track with our gown timeline on pages 66–67.

A subsector of the above industry, couture shops are also owner-operated. They are generally found in major cities and carry exclusively designer labels with higher-end prices. These are specialty shops that order new gowns cut specifically for particular measurements and are full-service. But remember, this level of quality and customer service comes at a high cost. Call ahead and ask if shops carry mother-of-the-bride gowns (inquire about the price range so you won't be surprised), and find out if appointments are required. If you go this route, consider a custom-gown designer that offers one-of-a-kind gowns, uniquely created for its customers, in all sizes. Find a designer whose vision you appreciate, as it will be a collaborative effort. But in the end, you'll have a gown like no one else's.

Nationwide bridal chains manufacture, import, and sell their own private-label gowns, which means that the style selection here can be more limited than in other types of stores. Prices most likely will be lower than at independent bridal shops, but so might be the quality of services. Before you buy, ask about the time required for on-site alterations.

Like bridal chains, good department stores also offer beautiful selections (though they're not usually labeled as mother-of-the-bride gowns) in their evening-wear departments. There's no rule stating you must buy a dress designated specifically for an MOB—but it's a good starting place and lets you garner a sense of what's appropriate. Particular sizes can be transferred from store to store or specially ordered, and alterations usually are available.

If you're looking for a real deal, check out outlet shops. They are self- or reduced-service, and they might or might not offer on-site alterations. Generally, moms who shop these stores should expect to buy off the rack and to take the gown home when it is purchased. Styles might be a mix of discontinued national brands and privately labeled merchandise sold at reduced prices. The real trouble with this route is alterations—if you don't have a seamstress with whom you've worked before, ask your friends.

YOUR SMART-SHOPPING TIMELINE FOR CUSTOM-MADE GOWNS

EIGHT MONTHS BEFORE THE WEDDING
❑ Get a sense of what's out there. Go online; buy wedding magazines.
❑ Sit down with your daughter to discuss the dress; start shopping.

SIX MONTHS BEFORE
❑ Order your gown. Make sure the following details are written on your receipt:
- Designer name
- Style number or name
- Size or measurements the salon is sending to the manufacturer
- Approximate delivery date
- How many fittings (if any) are included in the price
- How much money you still owe for the gown
- Amount of your deposit, and that it's marked "paid"

FIVE MONTHS BEFORE
❑ Call the salon to confirm the delivery date.
❑ Decide which accessories—shoes, lingerie, jewelry, wrap, gloves, outerwear, and bag—you need (or want!), and shop for them.
❑ If you plan to lose weight before your wedding, do so before your fittings begin. Once fittings are under way, try to maintain your weight.

FOUR TO FIVE WEEKS BEFORE
❑ Have your first fitting. Invite your daughter or one of your mother-of-the-bride maids (make sure she's eagle-eyed!) to come along. Bring your undergarments and accessories, too, so you can see the whole look. Make sure that
- the hem of a full-length gown skims the tops of the toes of your shoes.
- you can move comfortably.
- the dress stays in place as you move.
- there is no obvious wrinkling, bunching, or pulling.
❑ Continue to schedule fittings until you are completely satisfied.
❑ Learn about the dress. Find out how to banish last-minute wrinkles. Should you use an iron? On what setting? Is steaming a better option? And what if you spill something on it? Are there certain products you should or shouldn't use?

THREE WEEKS BEFORE

❏ Schedule a day and time to pick up your dress. We suggest you try it on one last time, no matter what the salon says, especially if it's been a while since your last fitting. We all know stress affects our appetites, and you don't want any last-minute surprises.

ADVICE ON ACCESSORIES

It's no secret that accessories help pull together your look. Splurge on truly comfortable shoes that match the shade of your gown, and treat yourself to a special purse to complete your ensemble for this important day. But before you head to the safe deposit box for your heirloom jewels, consider the style of the wedding and the look of your dress—especially if it has pearls, beads, or sequins. With black-tie ball gowns, you can get away with pretty much anything—even your most expensive jewels. But you don't want to overwhelm your look and come across like you just robbed a jewelry store—pick one eye-catching piece (a diamond brooch, silver bracelet, sapphire drop earrings) that suits your gown and accentuates your best feature. Complement a strapless dress with a great necklace; add some wrist candy to your sleeveless gown with a gorgeous bracelet; continue a high-necked look with sparkling earrings. Pass this advice (and maybe some of your jewels) on to your daughter. For brides, simplicity is key. She wants all eyes on her bridal glow, not her pearl choker.

[DRESS DON'TS]

Suffice it to say, mothers of the bride have to be careful (beyond wearing anything in the white/ivory/blush family). Try to avoid these moves:

- Perfectly matching the bridesmaids' dresses. You don't want it to seem that you were dying to be part of that party.

- Picking a dress that you would have worn when you were your daughter's age— for example, anything super-short or super-trendy.

- Sporting prints, stripes, or any bold pattern, which will just draw attention to your wedding wear. Stick with solid colors in deep shades.

- Discounting the dress code. Dressing too formally will only make your guests feel underdressed and uncomfortable.

BEAUTY BLUEPRINT

YOUR PAMPERING PLAN

Discovering the right dress is only half the battle in looking incredible on your daughter's wedding day. You also want to perfect your look and leave your friends wondering just how you turned back that clock. And, naturally, your hair and makeup must hold up for hours under heat, stress, and many happy tears.

Take Care of Your Hair

Start scheduling beauty services many months before the wedding. It takes a couple of really good haircuts to get your locks ready. If you're happy with your hairstylist, speak with him or her about how you wish your hair to look on the big day. That way, he can "train" your hair, prepping it for that specific style. As for your color, you don't want your highlights to be too fresh at the wedding—so schedule your final cut and color at least two weeks in advance of the date.

Perfect Your Skin

Avoid facials or chemical peels (or even Botox!) close to the event—you never know if your skin might react badly to a treatment. Instead, get back the supple skin of youth by starting healthful habits now. For most people, these should include washing your face twice a day with lukewarm or cool water (hot water evaporates moisture from surface cells, prematurely aging skin) and applying a moisturizer with a sunscreen afterward. A dermatologist can give you specific instructions on products you should use and how often to use them.

Don't skip sleep. Your body requires a minimum of eight hours of rest to rebuild and repair itself. During that time, it sheds dead skin cells, flushes out toxins and excess water, and regulates its natural moisture levels (among other things). Deprive yourself of sleep, and expect to see dull skin, dark circles, and puffiness.

Since your skin reflects how well you take care of yourself, an overabundance of smoking and drinking can also leave you with a pallid complexion. Cigarettes and alcohol both restrict oxygen circulation throughout your body, so your skin doesn't get the nutrients it needs to look healthy and supple. Drinking water and exercising, however, can help to increase circulation and flush out toxins. Basically, if you take good care of your hair and skin now, the wedding day will be easy.

BIG-DAY BEAUTY

If you can afford it, we strongly suggest that you have a professional do your hair and makeup on the big day—mostly to spare yourself the extra stress of having to do it yourself. You might be able to hire a makeup artist through the salon that does your hair—many offer makeup applications. An added bonus: Some salons offer a discount if you have them do both your makeup *and* your hair.

Talk to your daughter. Will a stylist or makeup artist come to the place where you will all get ready? Does she expect that you'll use the same person? You might want to have a different professional on hand for yourself, your mom, your other children, and maybe important aunts. That will ensure that the bride gets full attention.

Be sure to follow in your daughter's footsteps—set up a consultation first. Many professionals charge a small consultation fee, and later a separate wedding day fee. Others charge only one price up front, slightly higher than a wedding day fee, and offer a free consultation as part of the package. Caution: The problem with the latter plan is that you sign on with a stylist before you've had a chance to critique him or her—it's not "free" if you hate the results and need to find someone else.

You can also find a great makeup artist through local department stores. If you have a favorite makeup counter, head there for a free makeover. When you find what you like, ask the salesperson if she does any outside makeup work. (Who doesn't like extra cash?) She might be willing to come to you on the wedding day, or, if not, to set aside an appointment at the counter on the morning of the wedding.

After you've made all your plans with your professional, keep this in mind: You know your face better than anyone else does. Don't get talked into something you absolutely hate. You will have to live with your look (via pictures) for the rest of your life.

If you do your own hair and makeup, keep a few things in mind:

o Since you're not preparing for a day at the office, make sure you do a trial run.

o Practice on your face in all kinds of light—outside, inside, daytime, nighttime.

o Have someone take a few pictures of you so that you can get a well-rounded idea of how your makeup comes out on film. More makeup is always needed for photos—you don't want to seem gaunt or washed-out on camera.

o Don't be afraid to ask for help. Head to a makeup counter anyway and grab a few application tips from the salespeople there.

LOOK FABULOUS ON FILM

A professional photographer should know all the tricks of the trade to make you and your family look great in the photos—that's what you're paying for. But keep these tips in mind to light up the lens:

o Don't have a camera face-off. Standing square to the camera can make you look wide. Instead, turn your body slightly for a slimmer look. Figure out your "good" side and position yourself properly so it's most prominent.

o Banish that perma-grin look by resting your tongue behind your upper row of teeth. This relaxes your cheeks and gives you a more natural-looking smile.

o Stand up straight. It's that simple.

o No sparkly makeup; it interacts badly with light.

o Want to avoid a double chin? Stretch your neck and stick out your head slightly more than you normally would.

o Place one of your legs in front of the other, then put your weight on the leg that's in back. You'll wind up with your hips tilted away from the camera—super slimming!

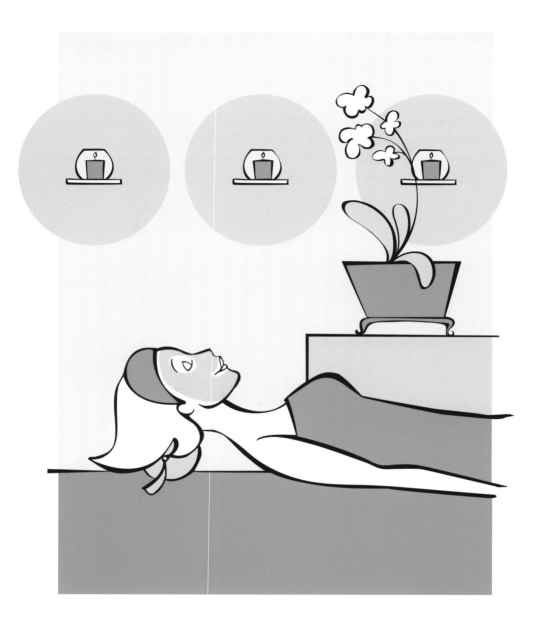

Even with the dress of your dreams, gorgeous designer shoes, and the perfect pocketbook, beauty really does come from the inside out, as corny as that sounds. And that starts with exercise. Toning up is not the only benefit of an exercise routine—it helps to alleviate wedding stress, gives your skin a healthy glow, and boosts your confidence. Exercise endorphins really do exist! If you haven't worked out in years, start off slow; walking is a great way to get the body moving and can even be a good time to socialize. Enlist one of your mother-of-the-bride maids (we're betting they want to get in shape for the big day, too!) and start a steady walking routine together. Finding a workout buddy is the best method to help yourself stick to a schedule and make the time fly by.

If you're already a steady exerciser, keep it up. For a change of pace, tailor your workouts to your dress style. Concentrate on your arms for a strapless gown or work on your calves for a knee-length number. We're sure you'll see a difference in how you look in the dress. Remember: Once you have your first dress fitting, don't diet or exercise excessively. Otherwise, alterations could be a nightmare.

Once you have all the wardrobe and body details down, be sure to try on your entire outfit long before the wedding. You don't want to find that your clutch clashes with your shoes moments before you head to the ceremony. In the end, feeling confident and comfortable in your ensemble trumps everything else, and it is the real secret to looking fabulous.

⌈ F O R G E T - M E - N O T S ⌉

If you'll get ready for the wedding away from home, it's easy to get stressed out when packing up your stuff for the big day. Refer to our checklist to make sure you've covered all the little elements:

- ❏ Dress and shoes
- ❏ Undergarments and extra pairs of pantyhose (don't wear hose with open-toed shoes)
- ❏ A purse that fits tissues and touch-up makeup: powder, lipstick, and gloss
- ❏ Jewelry: necklace, bracelet, earrings, and ring, and hair accessories

PARTY PRIMERS

SURE, YOU'VE GOT A WEDDING TO THINK ABOUT, but that tremendous celebration comes only after countless other gatherings (many of them ladies-only affairs) that are meant to gear up everyone for the big day. Some parties are traditionally meant to honor your daughter—the bridal shower, the bachelorette party— while others, such as the rehearsal dinner and the day-after brunch, extend the wedding's fun weekend vibe. Your role in planning these events varies tremendously— in many cases, your involvement is limited to attendance. But one thing's certain: They're a great time for friends and family to get together and bond over the couple you all adore so much.

In this chapter, we first provide you the entertaining essentials for those events (such as the shower) in which you'll assume a greater role. Next, we give you fun ideas for new party traditions to start; ways to help with the bachelorette party; and, finally, pointers on how to sit back and enjoy the rehearsal dinner. After all, you've earned it!

THE BRIDAL SHOWER

Traditionally, the prewedding shower was a time for women to converse about marriage, men, children, and what it takes to keep a home. It was also a time to "shower" the bride-to-be with gifts to bring to that new happy home. According to legend, the first bridal shower took place in the Netherlands when a young woman intended to marry a poor miller against her father's wishes; the girl's friends presented her with gifts, since she was refused a dowry. These days, bonding and gift-giving (as well as tremendous amounts of female fawning) are still on the main course, but men slowly are being incorporated into the celebration. We know this sounds rather progressive, but coed showers give the groom a chance to be a part of the party (and modern grooms are all about inclusion). Your daughter can also include other men who are crucial to her life: her father, brothers, or even male best friends. Consider who's throwing the shower before you decide on a his-and-hers shower; if her aunts are at the helm, a ladies' lunch might be more appropriate. You can always invite the men to arrive a little before the party's end to say hello (and load up the car with presents!). And there's no rule that says your daughter can't be showered more than once.

WHO HOSTS THE PARTY?

Typically it's the maid of honor, her bridesmaids, your daughter's aunts, or even your best friends. Customarily, the mother of the bride never throws the shower. That's often perceived as a rather gauche tactic to get your friends and family members to give your daughter gifts. But as you've probably learned by now, when it comes to weddings, there's plenty of rule bending. There's a good chance you'll be highly involved in planning it anyway, especially if one of your daughters is in the wedding party or if the bride's attendants (who usually do the honors) are scattered across the country. Our motto? Pitch in with the planning, but don't label yourself the host. Just check with the maid of honor (and perhaps also your daughter) to make sure she's comfortable with your involvement, since it's really her show. Follow her lead to make sure you don't step on each other's toes.

WHO MAKES THE LIST?

As in engagement party etiquette, it is strictly a faux pas to invite anyone to the shower who won't be invited to the wedding. The basic guest list should include your daughter's attendants, her closest female friends and relatives, and your soon-to-be son-in-law's mom, sisters, and other close female friends and family. From there, the size of the party really depends on who's throwing the event, where it's held, and if there are any budget considerations (which there usually are!).

If your daughter's future in-laws live far out of town, don't be surprised if one of the MOG's friends or family members also throws your daughter a shower. Her guest list probably will include her local friends and family who couldn't or wouldn't make it to the bride's-side shower. You, of course, will be invited as well.

[FUN SHOWER THEMES]

Eating, drinking, and opening presents are the only mandatory ingredients for a shower. But it's easy to add some spice to the traditional cake-and-champagne brunches or standard recipe-collecting lunches by planning around a theme. Here are some unique ideas:

Sex in the kitchen. Don't be frightened off by the provocative name. This party showers brides with both useful cookware and sassy bedroom wear. Instruct guests to bring their favorite recipe for an ethnic or gourmet dish and one of the rarer ingredients needed to make it (saffron for the perfect chicken soup; yam noodles for Korean *jap chae;* dried porcini mushrooms for an Italian risotto; and so on), along with a beautiful item of lingerie. You can use this as an opportunity to hand off a special book of fun family recipes.

Flower shower. Invite guests with a lovely floral note card and decorate the house with big bunches of single varieties of flowers placed in the type of tin buckets favored by florists. Ask in your local florist to teach the group a few flower-arranging tips so they can create their own arrangements. Serve whatever you like—watercress sandwiches or chicken salad—but garnish everything with edible flowers. If the couple already has their own home, you can give them a flowering tree to plant in their yard.

Celebrate the circle. Herald your daughter's entrance into the "circle of life" by celebrating the shape itself. Invite guests on round note cards; decorate the house with round Asian lanterns; and use pretty paper plates. Oh, and wear polka dots. As for what to serve, anything round is fair game: quiche, bagels, doughnuts, chocolate crepes, beef medallions, potato pancakes. . . . Consider rounding out your daughter's china collection by handing down your own.

Beauty bash. For the bride who loves to be pampered, a calming day of beauty could be just what the doctor ordered. Serve a spa-approved meal—salad, grilled chicken, green tea—and hire a manicurist to give quickie nail treatments. Spoil your daughter with a spa package gift certificate to use before the wedding day.

WHEN SHOULD YOU HAVE IT?

Timing for the shower really depends on everyone's availability. It can take place six months or two weeks before the wedding day; the only rule is that it comes after the engagement party and before the big day.

If the host chooses to throw a surprise shower, her fiancé is a good person to contact when selecting a date. After all, he probably knows her daily whereabouts better than anyone else does. Traditionally, showers are weekend afternoon affairs—think ladies' lunch again. But almost anything goes. Some bridesmaids look at the shower as a prelude to the bachelorette party and therefore host a cocktail-hour shower before going out and celebrating your daughter's last weeks of singleton life. This is especially popular when many guests are from out of town—combining prewedding parties on the same weekend alleviates some travel stress.

DIVVYING UP DUTIES

Everyone knows that bridal showers are really about watching the bride open presents with delight. But be sure the bridal party is aware of their gift-time duties. Designate someone (generally the maid of honor) to keep track of who gave what so it will be a cinch for the bride to write her thank-yous (if the maid of honor is busy with hosting duties, pick up this task yourself); create a team to streamline the sometimes tedious present-opening session by loosening wrapping paper and tape; and pick one crafty attendant to gather ribbons from the gifts to make the traditional ribbon bouquet that the bride will carry at the rehearsal.

During this gathering of cake, champagne, and general merriment, you might feel as if you have no part in showering your daughter. Don't. There are countless special things you can do for the bride as her mom. Seize this opportunity in the company of female friends and family to toast your daughter with words from the heart—it's a safe place to let out your sentimental feelings. You could also bring a photo album of your daughter taken during those awkwardly funny teenage years. If you feel artsy, photocopy some of the more precious shots to create placemats for the tables. Or start a "words of wisdom" journal for her: Buy a blank journal (in her wedding colors?) and christen the first page with mom-to-daughter marriage advice. Then pass the book to all the ladies in the room. We're sure they'll have plenty to add!

A REVAMPED REGISTRY

The bride and groom probably have already envisioned their dream registry, right down to the board games and bath mats—or they might think they have all the household essentials that they need. Tread lightly here. The registry might be one area where the bride and groom really want complete autonomy. Your job is just to spread the word; let your friends and family know where they're registered. It's totally tacky to list this information on the invitation, so use your mom power to make it known.

Near the time of the shower, figure out what, if anything, you will hand down to her. Maybe *your* wedding china, an antique sterling silver server, or monogrammed linens (she might be keeping her last name!). The shower is the perfect opportunity to present her with these sentimental gifts. Or go for the gusto and take care of some big-ticket item on her registry, such as a vacuum cleaner or espresso machine.

If your daughter does turn to you for your expert opinion, show her how hip you are with these five registering rules.

- Don't register for the life you'll live in twenty years. It's impossible to pinpoint how your tastes may change.

- Go beyond the five-piece place setting. A charger plate can turn dinnerware into something dramatic.

- Think beyond ordinary uses. Martini glasses as dessert bowls?

- Bring inherited dinnerware with you when you register to coordinate the look.

- Double up on practical items. Salad forks are far more useful than soupspoons.

THE BACHELORETTE PARTY

Typically, moms try to avoid this all-girls night out. Depending on your daughter's demeanor, mass amounts of alcohol and fun flirtatious games might be involved. Although you might feel that you have a super-tight relationship with your daughter, check on her comfort level if you ask to attend this event. Most important, don't be offended when you're not invited at all! Even though she might be a perfectly proper young lady, her friends might want to cook up something special for her, such as revealing games about her intimate relations with your son-in-law-to-be and gag gifts that center on possible honeymoon antics. Having Mom around could diminish the fun factor, let alone make you uncomfortable.

If you're worried about the wild night, it's OK to ask your daughter or the maid of honor if they've arranged for a designated driver or a limo. But remember, she's older than she was at her prom—you can't expect her to call you and check in every two hours.

Instead, show her that you care—and that you think the racy tradition is fun for her—by sending along a bottle of champagne with the maid of honor. Or, since more brides are having destination bachelorette parties or elaborate nights on the town (the costs of which are her bridesmaids' responsibility), perhaps you can make a little contribution. Offer to pay for the first round of drinks, or surprise the bride by sending a cake emblazoned with a photo of her as a little girl. See, moms can join in the fun, too.

THE BRIDAL LUNCHEON

The day before the wedding, the bride, her attendants, and female family members sometimes gather for a bridal luncheon hosted by the bride and meant to show her thanks for putting up with her all these hectic months. But don't expect your daughter's bridal party to be thrilled by the idea. Most women probably will have to work on that day, and feeling obligated to attend can increase their stress levels, unless it's a destination wedding at which everyone will gather a couple of days before the wedding anyway. If your daughter does choose to show her appreciation via a bridal luncheon, consider giving her a little something special in return, such as the wedding night peignoir, a custom-made photo album of her prewedding years, or a handwritten note for her to open after the big day. Otherwise, a super-indulgent trip to a spa for you, your daughter, and her sisters can take the place of a formal luncheon. And, to be honest, massages, manicures, and pedicures are just what the wedding doctor ordered.

Or suggest a last-minute mother-daughter luncheon to unwind and talk about the past, her future, and the big day. If your daughter doesn't seem thrilled by this gesture, don't worry—you can always take a posthoneymoon rain check. You need to be sensitive to her needs right now, as pressing as yours might feel. She is caught up in the future— and you're probably feeling very sentimental about the past. Try to judge if she needs to vent now, or whether your invitation to lunch will feel like a burden.

THE MOTHER-OF-THE-BRIDE MAIDS' LUNCHEON

Remember those ladies who have been by your side, listening to you rant and rave about the mixed-up wedding world? Why not start a new tradition and take them out to lunch? Thank them for all their support and help and for being great friends. Let this be a time for you to completely unwind—you don't have to worry about setting your daughter off with completely innocent remarks. You could also give your "maids" a little token of appreciation. It doesn't have to be anything extravagant; a monogrammed makeup bag will amply demonstrate your gratitude. Other ideas include a flowering plant, theater tickets, or a custom-embroidered "Mother-of-the-Bride Maid" T-shirt.

Remember, a luncheon doesn't have to mean lunch at a restaurant. Getting the ladies together is your main mission. Why not host . . .

- A day at the spa. Wash away any wedding woes with manicures, pedicures, and other pampering treatments.

- Cocktails—a true girls' night out. Remember your wilder years with martinis at a local watering hole.

- A shopping spree. Hire a chauffeur-driven car to take you to the nearest urban shopping mecca, and help your crew pick out fabulous outfits for the rehearsal dinner.

THE REHEARSAL DINNER

Most likely, your party-planning skills will finally get a rest for the rehearsal dinner. The groom's family traditionally takes care of the night-before party, which leaves you with a moment to simply enjoy being the mother of the bride. But you're not completely off the hook. You must supply your daughter's future in-laws with a guest list that's within their constraints. Ask your daughter what they have in mind for the rehearsal dinner and how many people you are allowed to invite. The must-have list should include immediate family, wedding-party members and their spouses/significant others, and the parents of any child attendants (inviting the children themselves is optional). Promptly provide the MOG with your complete list, including addresses—it's not a good idea to start off your relationship with them by making them feel that they need to bug you.

Keeping this in mind, you might also ask that many of your out-of-town guests be invited to the rehearsal dinner. But if the groom's parents want the event to be an intimate affair, suggest that they host the rehearsal dinner two nights before the wedding day (Thursday, for a Saturday wedding), and then together you can throw a casual cocktail party for out-of-towners on Friday night. Bottom line: It's their party and their call. You must be sensitive to any possible economic difference; they will do what they can afford. If they want to keep party numbers down, there's no reason you can't arrange a dinner for your guests someplace across town.

Now, if your daughter's future in-laws start making excessive requests of you (e.g., that you make the place card holders, help cover the cost of champagne, or scout potential caterers), try to keep your cool. Wait a little while before responding to their wishes—go for a walk to get some fresh air or postpone your discussion until the next day if possible. This will give you time to think through the issues and you'll be able to come back to the table calm and ready to deal with the situation. Be sure to ask questions instead of making accusations—why do they want your input on the caterer? Maybe their son loves your cooking and they wanted to include you in the decision?

Above all, make sure any rehearsal-dinner discussions go through the couple; they are your key to compromising with the in-laws. Remember, right before the big day is the time for the respective families to start coming together. In fact, you may want to start your interaction with the in-laws right by giving them a tiny "welcome to the family" gift. Just don't go overboard—you won't want them to feel uncomfortable if they don't have something to give in return. Some ideas are a picture frame holding your favorite shot of the couple, a bottle of wine, or, to start on a light note, *Meet the Parents* on DVD.

Certain situations might increase your participation in this event. When the couple is hosting the wedding themselves, consider planning the rehearsal dinner in tandem with the future in-laws. This egalitarian approach eliminates many guest-list issues, as both parties have a stake in the event. Or, if the wedding will be in your hometown and the groom's family lives far away, take it upon yourself to offer them a wealth of suggestions of places to host the event. In the end, a relaxed and open-minded attitude only makes for a better wedding.

THE DAY-AFTER BRUNCH

Yes, we know . . . you still have to get through the wedding before reliving the events at the next-day brunch. But you need to start planning it now. A postwedding brunch, typically thrown by the bride's family, is a great way to wind down the festivities. If they aren't already honeymoon-bound, your daughter and son-in-law can enjoy a final opportunity to thank their guests and spend a little more time with faraway friends and family. The brunch is usually attended by the couple's families and any wedding guests who are still in town, but feel free to include attendants and friends. A close friend, such as one of your mother-of-the-bride maids, can even host this event. Basically, anything goes.

A buffet best suits this event—you'll want to create a flowing environment since you won't have control over everyone's comings and goings due to their travel schedules. If the wedding is in your hometown, consider inviting everyone to your house (you will probably have to call in a caterer—there's no need for the MOB to scramble eggs five hours after the wedding!). And consider transportation issues: Will you need valet parking to accommodate all the cars? How will people without a car get to the event? You could call up a local restaurant or hotel to host the affair. The increased costs might be worth the added ease.

Keep your guests abreast of all the details by either inserting a card into the wedding invitations of the guests you would like to invite or sending a completely separate mailing. The cards can be as formal or as casual as the brunch itself. If it's very casual, inviting your guests via telephone or e-mail is completely appropriate. Here's an example of standard invitation wording:

Please join us for
Brunch
Sunday, July 24
11 o'clock in the morning
The Does
111 Main Street
New York, NY
Regrets only by July 10
(212) 555-5555

If many of your guests are staying at hotels, consider coordinating the brunch's starting time with a typical check-out time, such as 11 A.M. Be aware that you and your guests might feel a little sluggish (an all-night celebration can take its toll). For a successful brunch, sometimes simple is best. Serve up omelets, French toast, waffles, pancakes, scones, croissants, bagels, coffee, and juices—mimosas and Bloody Marys are also the perfect final touch for the wedding's festive feel.

Use the centerpieces from the wedding for décor, and consider toasting the newlyweds, including a final thanks to guests who traveled from out of town. It's a great idea to have pictures on hand, too, to remind guests of just how fabulous the wedding was. If possible, take disposable cameras or a friend's film from the night before to a one-hour photo developer in the morning. Or, better yet, grab one of the bride and groom's friends' digital cameras and ask them to upload all their pictures onto a laptop—just make sure they first edit out those late-night antics.

THE BIG DAY AND
BEYOND

The day of the wedding is sure to be both a sweet and a sad time for you. Your daughter will be on the brink of becoming a married woman and starting her own family, the ultimate emotion explosion for any mom. So take advantage of your last moments with your single sweetheart. Your aim in the twenty-four hours before the wedding is to enjoy yourself and do whatever you can to help her enjoy herself, too. Give her some warm words of encouragement and tell her how much you love her. And remind her to take pleasure in every minute because, before she knows it, the band will announce their last song.

Probably you, too, will be in a fever of anticipation for this party that you've worked so hard to help perfect, and you'll be anxious that everything go off without a hitch. From the ceremony to the reception, here are some surefire strategies to help you make the most of the main event when it finally comes. And we couldn't forget about dealing with the days after the wedding—and neither will you, with our tips on preserving wedding memories long after the cake has been cut.

BEFORE THE FESTIVITIES

THE FINAL COUNTDOWN

The last moments before the wedding will be a raging storm of emotion for everyone involved. You'll be rushing around trying to make sure everyone is accounted for, so there's bound to be some breakdowns. But you've handled it before. Remember the terrible twos? All brides lash out at their mothers, and your role, now more than ever, is to be her supporter, her comforter, her island of calm in a hectic sea. Listen to what she is saying, assuage her frayed nerves—and make sure you've hired a professional day-of consultant.

You might have brought a wedding planner on board long ago, but even if you and your daughter have assumed that task, a day-of coordinator can be a lifesaver. What's expected of the coordinator can vary, but basically her job is to ensure that the wedding goes off smoothly and that all your professionals show up on time. You supply her with all the necessary vendor numbers and addresses, so once the big day rolls around, all you have to worry about is looking your most gorgeous and getting ample beauty sleep beforehand. Don't know where to find this ultimate organizer? Ask a local wedding planner for a recommendation. Her company might even offer the service. If not, tell your daughter to ask her married friends for leads.

After the rehearsal dinner, you'll want to bring the bride home for a last-minute bonding session. It's a good idea to take some time to reassure her that everything is in place and that there's nothing to fear. You could ask her what's on her mind. Many parents choose this time to give the bride a special present, such as family jewels to wear the next day or a good-luck charm. Don't be offended if she doesn't wear what you've given her—chances are she has already planned her outfit down to every last detail. Sleep will probably be hard to come by on this night, but you can rest assured that you and your daughter have spent the final hours enjoying her soon-to-be-wedded bliss.

GETTING TO THE CHURCH ON TIME

Even though you (and your daughter) might not sleep a wink the night before the wedding, you'll need to muster the energy to start the day right. Don't under-estimate the amount of prep time you and she both need to get ready—always add an extra hour to your estimate.

Plan to serve up a good, solid breakfast for everyone in the house, because this might be your last square meal for many hours. It's not the time to show off your renowned overnight French toast recipe—there's too much to tackle. A simple fruit salad and cereal might be your best breakfast friends. Or, if time allows, maybe you can go out for a nice leisurely breakfast.

One of your day's toughest jobs will be to balance giving your daughter time to collect her thoughts and banish wedding jitters with efficiently moving her through her morning of beautification. Depending on the time of the wedding, you might have room for some day-of activities. Don't count on this for ceremonies that start before 4 P.M. But if you've planned a 7 P.M. showtime, you can schedule morning manicures and pedicures or a much-needed massage. Just keep your eye on the time.

Above all, don't be a minute late for your hair and makeup appointments. You must get your gorgeous self and the blushing bride to the (insert here: church, synagogue, garden) on time and ensure it's all smiles down the aisle. If you and your daughter are sharing a makeup artist and hairstylist, make sure you have coordinated the timing to a T. Establish who's going first, and be ready for your appointment. Don't sacrifice a perfect coif to bad planning. The photographer will probably want to capture some getting-ready shots, so it's a good idea for you to get fully dressed before the bride does. And make sure the dressing area looks presentable for the photos—it's always chaotic when women get dressed for a big event, and ever so easy for mascara-smeared tissues and other rubbish to collect.

When your daughter's hair has been set and her makeup done to perfection, it is time for her final bridal transformation: putting on the wedding gown. It's usually the maid of honor's role to handle the intricacies of the gown, such as arranging the bustle and train, but it's always a good idea to be her backup. Some quick tips: Big gowns are set on the floor and stepped into, so you might want to lay down a sheet

to keep her precious dress clean. Second, leave time to fasten the dress—the ones with buttons take forever. Make sure someone (one of the bridesmaids, perhaps) is assigned to carry the train around the house and into the car—it's way too easy to catch that fine handiwork on something and get it dirty. Finally, suggest that your daughter take one last toilet trip (flashbacks, anyone?) and limit any food or drink once she's in the dress. We know it sounds harsh, but we've heard too many Diet Coke-spill horror stories. If she really needs nourishment, wrap a towel around her and feed her just as in her baby days.

Also, make sure you have an emergency kit on hand to fix last-minute dress disasters; gather together a sewing kit, extra pantyhose, safety pins, double-sided tape, and Shout wipes. This might be the height of nervousness for your daughter—showing her how calm you are (even if you're not!) can help soothe her fears. Be sure to smile, laugh, and tear up. Did we mention you should wear waterproof mascara? Then send her to the ceremony.

⌈MOM'S EMERGENCY KIT⌉

You're focused on making sure your daughter has everything she could possibly need, but what about you? Don't forget to pack these essentials:

- A snack

- Tissues or a handkerchief

- Blotting papers for shiny skin

- Lipstick—if the makeup artist used a special shade, ask if you can purchase it

- Band-Aids, for those killer heels

- Aspirin

- Breath mints or gum

WEDDING DAY SCHEDULE

To prepare for the mayhem before her marriage, review this day-of-the-wedding schedule and keep it handy—feel free to adjust the time frames to suit your needs. This is based on a 6:30 P.M. ceremony.

DAY OF THE WEDDING

8:30 A.M. Gently wake up the bride. While she's shaking off sleep, prepare a light, energy-enhancing breakfast.

8:45 A.M. Check a weather report to confirm what's in store. Call the wedding-day team to make any necessary adjustments.

9:00 A.M. Take time out. Indulge in something peaceful and relaxing—maybe a massage?

10:15 A.M. Hit the showers. Keep the cell or cordless phone close at hand, just in case.

12:00 NOON Bridesmaids arrive with their dresses and emergency equipment in hand—extra stockings, hairspray, sewing kits, clear nail polish, bobby pins, dental floss, and tissues.

12:30 P.M. Hair and makeup stylists arrive. You should be first on the get-ready list so you can help your daughter get into her dress.

1:30 P.M. Time for the bridesmaids to take their beauty turns.

2:30 P.M. Lunchtime—something simple but nourishing. Foods to avoid: salty snacks, caffeine, and booze.

3:15 P.M. The next two hours belong to your daughter. While she gets her hair and makeup done, take care of the dress and any additional steaming and pressing; have the bridesmaids inspect for loose threads and wrinkling areas.

4:00 P.M. Bouquets arrive and are distributed before photos. Photographer's assistant arrives to set up for pre-wedding photos.

5:00 P.M. Photographer arrives for shots of bride and bridesmaids primping and getting dressed, looking in the mirror, and other cool candids. You, your husband, the bride, and bridesmaids should be dressed and ready for camera action.

6:00 P.M. Depart for the ceremony site (of course, this depends on how far you have to travel).

SPECIAL WORDS FOR A SPECIAL MOMENT

Think ahead: As you and the bridal party gather outside the ceremony space, queuing up and exchanging anticipatory hugs, you might want to say something to your daughter that she'll remember forever. You've waited for this moment since the first time you laid eyes on her wrapped in that pink receiving blanket, but how can you possibly express yourself when she's about to walk down the aisle? The best and most eloquent way to ring true is to stay simple and be real, honest, and heartfelt.

Here's an idea: In a quiet moment, think about your daughter and the wedding and let your mind wander to her childhood. Chances are an appropriate favorite memory will float into your mind. Briefly describe it, tell her why you treasure it so, and link it to the day (perhaps it was the moment when you realized she'd make a wonderful wife and mother).

If you want to write something instead of saying it, find a favorite childhood photo of the two of you, jot a simple note on the back that she can read at a glance (something like "You turned into the woman I always dreamed you'd be" will do), and slip it into her bouquet to carry as her "something old." Or simply tell her she looks beautiful, that you love her, and that you're very happy for her. The more supportive you are now, the more she'll feel able to come to you if and when she needs to. Avoid uttering *any* clichés, especially "We're not losing a daughter; we're gaining a son-in-law," but you'll probably make her day by complimenting her soon-to-be-husband. Go ahead and tell her you love him, or just say you're overjoyed that she found the one.

WORDS OF WISDOM

Other cultures have created many special rituals that make the bride's and groom's families an important part of the ceremony. Get inspired by fun ways mothers and fathers around the globe show they care.

- If you really want your daughter to feel loved, consider surprising her with this Egyptian tradition (just don't stay for dinner): the bride's family cooks for the couple for a week after the wedding so the newlyweds can spend their time . . . relaxing.

- In South Africa, the parents of both bride and groom traditionally carried fire from their hearths to light a new fire in the newlyweds' hearth.

- Libation is a traditional African ceremony in which a family elder pours water on the ground in the four directions that the wind comes from, in remembrance and honor of the couple's ancestors.

- In Thailand, the mothers of the bride and groom walk to the altar to drape *puang malai*—flower garlands—around the couple's shoulders to wish them good fortune in their life together.

- Give your girl a gold coin to put in one shoe, have her dad give her a silver one for the other, and Swedish tradition says she'll never, ever have to do without.

- Two days before Sicilian weddings, relatives go to the new home of the bride- and groom-to-be and "make the bed." The mother of the bride puts money under her daughter's pillowcase, and the mother of the groom puts money under her son's. The bed is also dressed with Jordan almonds, and money is pinned to the sheets to bring prosperity and good fortune.

- In China and Japan, it is customary for the couple to present their parents with tea and sake, respectively, to represent the new family bond.

THE MAIN EVENT
CEREMONY ESSENTIALS

Even though most mothers of the bride are on the same emotional page, their ceremonial role varies tremendously among faiths. In Christian traditions, you are the last person seated before the bridal procession begins, and either your son or a special family member escorts you to the front row of the church's left side. It is there you wait for your husband (or whoever your daughter's escort might be) to join you. In Jewish celebrations, the mother and father of the bride both walk her down the aisle, and often remain under the huppah on either side of the rabbi. Talk to your daughter about how much she wants you to participate in the ceremony— sometimes parents perform readings or light candles. And then, before you know it, she will be kissing the groom and running down the aisle to celebrate.

THE INS AND OUTS OF THE RECEIVING LINE

If you're deliberating about whether to have a receiving line, consider this: You can skip this formality and rely on the more casual greet-them-as-you-see-them approach, but that might leave you and the bride and groom in a tailspin for the rest of the night, ducking out of conversations to say hello to people you haven't yet greeted. Even worse, inevitably you'll end up missing someone. Generally pulled together outside the ceremony space or during the cocktail hour, a receiving line is the easiest way to ensure your guests have a minute of face-to-face time with the bride and groom and get a chance to congratulate you! And that leaves you free to enjoy a dance or two later down the road.

Traditionally, the bride's parents, as hosts, head the receiving line and are first to greet guests, followed by the bride and groom and then the groom's parents. Many variations exist: some lines include the entire bridal party, space permitting, and even grandparents. Keep in mind that a huge receiving line can put guests in an awkward position, as they must find something to say as they go down the line and endure a long time commitment. Today, it's perfectly acceptable for the couple to stand alone, or with just their moms and dads, while whoever isn't included (such as the attendants) circulates among and welcomes the crowd during cocktail hour.

It can be easy to get caught up in conversation at such a big moment, especially when you haven't seen many guests in quite a long time. But as mother of the bride, you must be in constant control of the clock. You should welcome a hug or kiss and a simple congratulation from each person and move on. If someone wants to talk more, say, "I can't wait to come and chat with you later." Another great timesaver: Greet guests at once as a couple so you and your husband don't need to reiterate the warm wishes for each person.

[DEALING WITH AN EX]

If you and the bride's father are divorced, the best advice we can give you is to be gracious no matter what situation you find yourself in. Nothing disrupts a wedding (or your daughter's happiness) like a display of awkwardness or hostility between you and your ex.

BROACH THE TOPIC

It should go without saying that your daughter is allowed to involve her family in any way she wants, but it's also unfair for any of you to suffer through tense moments. So instead of skirting the issue with your daughter, open the door for conversations about how you can make each situation as comfortable as possible. For instance, your daughter can prepare ushers who direct your ex to his seat at the ceremony, and she can arrange reception seating accordingly. Or maybe she wants you to walk her down the aisle. You won't know until you ask.

STAND UP FOR YOURSELF

As for the receiving line, whether it's you or the groom's parents, divorced couples should not stand next to each other in line—even if they share hosting duties—since this gives the impression that you are still a couple, which can be awkward for guests who don't know. Instead, you should stand on one side of the bride and groom; the groom's parents come next, on the other side of the couple; then your daughter's father stands on their far side. For stepparents, let your daughter or son-in-law be the judge. If she has a good relationship with a stepparent, then by all means he or she should be included. Of course, that means the divorced couple (you and your ex) must be able to share this duty with civility and grace.

SAY CHEESE, PLEASE

Prepare a concrete plan for the family portraits. Plan out who will stand where. Let the photographer know your plans ahead of time. You can take a photo with the couple and one parent, then switch; in the group shot, place divorced parents on either side of their child; or abandon the formal photo altogether. Remember, these days anything goes.

DIVVY UP DUTIES

If the groom's parents are divorced and you want to welcome both his mother and father into the family while maintaining the peace, split up and tag-team with your husband while you mingle. He can keep good contact with the father of the groom while you charm the groom's mom.

RELISHING THE RECEPTION

HAVING FUN AS A HOST

Once your daughter is proudly wearing that wedding band, it's time to breathe, enjoy a glass of Chardonnay, and dance like proud parents should. Remember, if some kinks creep out during the night, that's just fine. We guarantee no one will even notice. Here is your fabulous plan to ensure you have fun as a host and secure some goodwill along the way.

Eat before you go. As we said earlier, there's a good chance that you'll be either too busy or too excited to take more than a bite or two once the time comes. And nothing makes it harder to handle stressful moments and socialize than a blood-sugar dip. We've heard of many moms who packed a healthful pick-me-up (almonds, energy bars) for nourishment on the way to the reception. And sample those tasty hors d'oeuvres you helped select. Even if you don't finish your main course, at least you'll have something in your stomach.

Give them something to talk about. Spend as much time as possible mingling and catching up with old friends and family members. Introduce people who you think might get along. A successful wedding is one that no one wants to leave and where everyone has fun. And if you're having fun, your guests will follow your lead.

Rely on your mother-of-the-bride maids. Remember them? Your own support network of attendants? It's time to put them to work again. As the bride's mom, you surely want to deal with every detail so your daughter doesn't have to. So, you might ask one friend to keep an eye on your frisky Uncle Jim or another to encourage people to dance. You get the picture. Relying on others for small roles can free you up to focus on the bigger stuff . . . and to enjoy yourself.

Have fun with your hubby. You've probably been so preoccupied with caring for your daughter that your darling spouse has been left hanging out to dry. Show him that all those months of planning were worth it, and cut a rug with him on the dance floor. Together, take a look at your daughter and congratulate each other on a job well done.

Kvell. Imagine this: The cake is late, Great-Aunt Martha is complaining that there have been too many toasts, and suddenly you feel a little frazzled. You'll have to stop. Breathe. Breathe again. Take in the beautiful room, the chattering guests. Notice how your daughter is smiling at your new son-in-law. Smile yourself as you revel in your pride and happiness. Spend one full minute letting these feelings wash over you. This is called *kvelling*, and, as a mom, you're naturally good at it. Then you'll be able to return to handling the details, feeling calmer and a whole lot less crazed.

Welcome the in-laws. Now that your two families are bonded together by this union, open your arms to them. Make sure you plan a dance with your new son-in-law; spend a moment or two with the groom's parents, swapping stories of preceremony jitters; and extend yourself to the groom's entire family. All it takes is a simple smile and a heartfelt hug.

Take a bathroom break. At some point in the night, head to the loo and make sure that your makeup still looks good, your hair is perfectly set, and you've got it all together. A brief bathroom respite in the middle of the reception could be just what you need to revive your glamorous look, boost your confidence, and help yourself keep mingling.

Skip the apologies. Worried that you'll have to say sorry to your husband's mother because her sister wasn't invited? Or apologize to Aunt Joan because your daughter hasn't managed to mail her thank-yous for the engagement gifts she gave her months ago? We have one word for you: don't. There is a time and a place for everything, and this isn't it. Instead, use your time with each guest to smile, graciously thank him or her for coming, and let it all go and have a good time together.

THE DISH ON DANCING

Every wedding has its own personality and flair, but some traditions are well worth copying. At some point in the night, after the bride and groom have christened the dance floor, the band or DJ will open the floor to special family dances: the all-important father-daughter dance, the mother-son dance, and the spin for both sets of parents. Get your song picks ready long before the big night, and make sure the band knows which song to play when. We know of one wedding band that mistakenly played "Sexual Healing" during the mother-son dance!

Now, your family might not fit this traditional order. Even if your husband is around, why not start your own trend with a mother-daughter dance? It's a wonderful moment for the two of you to catch up amid the spinning revelry. Often, the groom will ask his new "mom" (you!) to dance. You don't need to pick a special song for this moment; any slow tune will do. And if you're looking for a truly special sentimental touch, ask the band to play each set of parents' first dance songs at a certain time (the earlier the better).

TIPS ON TOASTING

Toasting (and more often roasting) also has a special place at every wedding—heartfelt words make guests feel welcomed and the couple elated. No one will raise an eyebrow if you don't grab the mike, but that missed opportunity can leave a tinge of regret. Generally speaking, the best man will kick things off at the dinner hour with a funny anecdote or sentimental story about how he realized your daughter was the perfect match for his best friend or brother. One of the bride's best friends might follow up, and even the groom's parents might want to honor the happy couple, especially if the rehearsal dinner was an intimate affair. You and your husband probably will address the newlyweds last. Obviously, you can schedule speakers however you wish, but this way you can give a final thank-you to the guests for coming, welcome your new son-in-law to the family, and leave the room resonating with your heartfelt words.

Decide with your husband how you want the toast to play out. While it's not strict tradition for the mother of the bride to speak, it's becoming more common. (Just clear it with your daughter first.) Maybe your husband's not the toasting type and wants to just stand by your side as you speak from both of your hearts. Or you can share the duties. Do whatever makes you both comfortable. Just remember the following:

1. Specifically address the bride and groom.
2. Prepare something to say—even a poem, a quote, or a traditional Irish toast. And be simple and quick; three minutes is tops.
3. But make it seem spontaneous. You don't want to whip out a ten-page essay on your daughter's love. Even if you've rehearsed your words, they will seem much more meaningful if they sound off the cuff and from the heart.
4. Start off lightheartedly; be sure to say something about how happy you are that your daughter has found such a wonderful man.
5. Include all the guests in the toast—don't share inside jokes that only your daughter will understand.
6. At the end, instruct guests to raise their glasses and take a sip of celebration. Too many people forget it's a toast, not a speech!

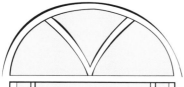

THE GRAND FINALE

You won't want to believe it, but at some point, the wedding will come to an end. Expect to be lavished with good-byes during the final hour. Per etiquette, it's perfectly acceptable for guests to leave once the cake has been cut. Your daughter and (wow!) son-in-law are probably set to exit the wedding in a proper send-off complete with sparklers, fireworks, or something equally earth-shattering and romantic. But make sure you leave time to settle the bill. First, days before the wedding, establish the tipping procedure at the reception space with the catering manager. Must you go around to individually present the bartenders and servers their tips? Or will he collect the balance and distribute it accordingly? You'll also have to check in with the band and photographer to make any necessary final payments.

Before you're out the door, do a last-minute room check for forgotten items, collect disposable cameras from the tables, and, if they haven't already been grabbed, collect the centerpieces—decoration for your home or next-day brunch, perhaps? It's a good idea to come prepared with boxes for all these items. Don't forget that there probably will be a table filled with wedding presents as well, and you won't want to leave them behind.

Once the party's over, there will still be so much more to the event. Even if you aren't bidding your guests adieu with a farewell brunch, welcome these post-wedding hours and create a memento to commemorate one of the best days of your life. Now put up your feet, reminisce, and smile—you pulled it all off with style.

TAKING IT ALL IN

After you've basked in the wedding glory, there are still some postwedding to-dos that will help you and your daughter preserve the memory of the magnificent day. Many couples choose to save the top tier of the wedding cake to eat on their one-year anniversary. Since your daughter might be honeymooning out of the country, take the first steps to ensure it will be edible in a year. First, make sure the reception site places the cake tier in a freezer-safe plastic container; then, when you get home, seal the cake tightly in plastic wrap (get out all the air, as that's what makes it go stale) and then two layers of tinfoil. Transfer the cake to her fridge when they get home.

Next, take steps to preserve her dress. Whatever you do, do not put the gown in a box in the attic—your daughter will open it years from now to find yellowing, moldy, deeply creased fabric that *her* daughter won't be too excited to resurrect, regardless of its nostalgic appeal. Instead, rely on gown-preservation specialists, who carefully clean wedding gowns and veils and then specially package them for maximum protection. Ask if they can repair any minor rips or tears. We don't know of a single gown that wasn't stepped on all night long.

Finally, think about preserving other mementos of the day. Look into freeze-drying her bouquet yourself or having a reputable company do it (you should drop it off no more than two days after the wedding); frame an invitation; or create a photo album from disposable-camera pictures taken at the wedding. These keepsakes will thrill your daughter. Another huge helper for your posthoneymoon daughter: Write thank-you notes to all the key vendors so she doesn't have to.

EPILOGUE

PLANNING A WEDDING IS NO SMALL FEAT. There are countless details to consider, personalities to please, and relationships to maintain. Keep yourself on track by remembering one thing: The day is meant for your daughter and her fiancé to show the world how much they love each other. She wants to welcome him into the family—your family—with a bang. So enjoy it! You'll spend months on an emotionally charged roller coaster with your daughter, talking on the telephone up to four times a day. And then it seems that it's over in a snap. Many mothers speak of the postwedding blues, but take solace in this: Your relationship with your daughter will never be better! She's bound to be grateful for all the hard work, love, and support you've showered on her throughout the planning process. Once she's out of the wedding bubble, she will see how amazing you were (and are!) at balancing that support with helping to get things done. The bottom line: She'll still be calling you four times a day—but this time, just to chat.

The brides at The Knot had plenty to share when we asked about their moms' roles in their weddings. Here's what they say they'll never forget.

"The night before the wedding, I was sitting on my bed crying my eyes out, trying to write a letter to her. She came into my room and asked why I was crying, and I showed her the letter, half-finished. She read it and said, 'Don't write any more. Everything you need to say, I already know.' The letter sits on her shelf to this day, half-finished in mid-sentence."— EMILY

"Plain and simple, she was there for me and was wonderful throughout the entire planning process. I couldn't have asked for anything more fabulous than that."— JENELLE

"She handled every last detail. I was worry-free before, during, and after the wedding!"— ERIN

"She listened to all my problems and complaints, no matter how minor or frivolous. She has given me awesome advice about being a wife, a partner, a mother, and a woman in general—but never unsolicited!"— AMOS

"My mom has been taking pictures for everything that we do. With them, she is creating a prewedding album so that I will have 'before' memories."— KELSEY

"She is being supportive and honest; that's what she does the best. That's why I love her."— CRYSTAL-DAWN

"She loves my groom like he's her own kid. (And when he visits, he gets put to work like her own kids, especially on stuff that you really need a tall guy like him for.) She cares for him as much as she does for me, including what's best for him."— KATE

"She stayed out of the planning process but was there if I needed anything. She said that she was staying out of it since it was our day. She didn't want it to be hers; she already had her wedding day!"— ANGELA

"Even though my mom didn't love the reception space my fiancé and I really wanted, she soon came on board and had a ton of ideas to make it look perfect. I couldn't have done it without her help!"— ANN

"The greatest thing that my mom did was give me a picture of my dad, her, my uncle, and me when my dad was in the army to carry in my bouquet. I lost my dad six years ago, so carrying the picture in my bouquet was like having my dad with me as I went down the aisle."— VICKI

"One tradition we've formed is going out for dinner and martinis after trips to the bridal shop. We have been out so much that I'm hoping they can squeeze me into my dress!"— JENNIFER

INDEX